I0143233

ISBN: 978-0-692-28377-6

Year 13

I once had a book that I dared not let anyone see.
I was afraid to let anyone in to know the real me.
There once was a time when there was silence before the words.
No need to introduce that which I wanted to remain obscure.
So I would talk into the mic only to say,

"Hello,

I am TCPoeto,

and this, is my poetry."

Hiding from the crowds with the lights in my eyes. Waiting and pining
to return home to my lines.
The lines of words marked in unlined pages. Dark spattering and
chicken scratch barely discernible as my body ages.
My stories becoming wrinkles in my face and in time. Smoothed over
with a calm countenance and a gentle reminder of the rhyme.
And I begin to digress as I attempt to regress to that place from which I
wrote to write again from the place in my mind seemingly so remote.
Hidden not just from a sea of new faces, but from myself as well as the
memory of
itself   it   erases.

Until I sit here before you once again trying to find just one more pen.
To fight the drying of the ink, and to not introduce these thoughts I
think.

To let them stand out on their own
                        for _you_ to decide from whence they've grown.

My pen has been silent so long.

Awake oh ye beast of burden and bear the brunt brutality of vocabulary as you vocalize volumes of voracious verbs, verbose but not forgotten as forlorn fingers foil fantasies forgiving memories and moments momentous and magical that musically adorn arduous ears. Ever eager, even when we wile away winter's weeping whispers of snow sneaking silently softly onto our open orifices opulent and orating.
Kiss the kinder kisser, of pages purloined of pretty prose pressed on fine papyrus in red ink intertwined intently inside content covers of cow's hide caressed with care curtailed not by nature's not knowing of our own natural intent. Intense moments carnalized on tongues tasting tantalizing tastes of speech. Guttural, gutsy, seemingly grand and gifted by the divines.

Divination through proclamation.

Speaking with sublimation, not subjugation as subliminally we dance in hopes to entrance and enthrall as we inherently enhance the enlightenment of all in our endeavors.
Speak softly, speak slowly but salivate and slacken jaws as jeers fall and jokes renounce recumbent's fates. Fear not the fall out, the fallacies and the phalluses. Let the phallic pen and its oozing tip tear out in time to its own rhythm, to its own rhyme.

Remember why you wrote and why you write this writ.

To remember that taste of tongue in cheek as others listen and opine upon our wit.

To shake the hands of a million people bare. To stare into their eyes as the coffers rise a dollar at a time. To tell them a story and see on their face their suspension of disbelief as emotions are evoked, and smiles are born. Torn from the pages marked in ink all colors of the rainbow. To know the past, the deeds and soon the fates of those once so low now rising in haste. Songs in verse once conversed in coffee shops and bars and clubs dark with minimal light. The darkness a boon in which we hide from sight the flaws of our caricatures and the defects in our characters. A dance, a play, a Broadway show we perform. The answers only questions in riddle form. No room for error, for no missteps. A dance macabre our words beget. With tongues soft and tantalizing shaping the ebb and flow, providing the means for new people to know ourselves and our deeds. Travels and travails sifting through the veils without the aid of Don Quixote's steed. Fighting windmills for a love divine. A love without recourse, a love for which we pine. Sometimes spineless we dream of those things naught. And long for them to be. The scent of sweet perfume on pillow tops do yet remain, the incense as the absence grows longer 'til we forget her name. The shadows of memories. Lovers long lost. A pot of gold from a kiss, imparted on the softest pink lips. The nectar so sweet, the taste so fine. A lover for tonight yet never and for all time. Simultaneous dreams beseeching the soul. Contradictions in terms and to never grow old. Emboldened hearts speaking a symphony. Tasting new tastes as fresh as an epiphany. The spark of light begging to be seen. The fruit we now call inspirational dreams. Darkness banished from a mind besieged with guilt. To have Proust's new eyes, to see the world we wished, built. Mortar and stone. Hands cracked from broken clay we build what we see from our imagination's play. Let the stories of that building reach high into the sky. Together we create new skylines. A light up night, a feast for the agape. The stories we speak soon to take shape into cities that wake. Early morning transits. The shuffling of feet. Traveling new roads, hearing new beats. Production but a reason to call our day done. Going out, or home, we search for our own fun. Hobbies and distractions for which we recreate. Dancing to dance, finding solitude to masturbate. Mental masturbation I call a stroke of genius. To think and to play in one's own mind hoping for the fruit of new ideas so sublime. Picturesque ideas sifting through a kaleidoscope. Shattered and fragmented we may call this art. Abstract by nature, metaphorical out of need. The best of the worst as our emotional creed.

Systematic Devaluation
of one's inner reluctance.
Shocking aspirations in self doubt
leading us to no conclusion.

Pens aimlessly wandering pages.
Mixed thoughts feeding emotions.
Words torn between voices.
Songs caught in the throat of orchestration.

Hands falling as eyes are glazed.
Hap-hazard omittance of the dazed.
Cherished tragedies of thrills unknown.
Hidden images of mysterious life not shown.

Desperate measures of pangs and loss.
Look inside at tangled webs. Who's the boss?
Cords pulling, thoughts pushing.
Hearts ripping in one smashed accord.

Again I ask who am I?

For I don't know.

Where is the origin of thought -
 the heart or the mind?
For I cannot find it nor discern
 whether it is original or the act of subjugation.
Why do I so often think of what I'm feeling
 and feel what I'm thinking?
What is that sharp pain and bitter taste in my dream?
 How does my phantasy know grief?
Many years it took to place thick callouses over my emotions.
 Thus what have I done to my God?
Have I shielded in my mind in place of shielding out agony?
 To place so much emphasis on intellect.
To drive away emotions. Who needs pain with reason?
 Yet to choose our emotions analytically.
Hand in hand don't they walk? Through dark passageways.
 The hallways of the mind, of enlightenment.
Locking the doors of that passageway has advanced maturity
 Yet stunted the surreal imagination.
Is imagination the child of mind (the masculine) and emotions (the
feminine)?
 Then in my abortion I have slaughtered the artist I have tried
to become.
I've suffocated my dream of dreaming with a mouthful of reason.
 Who is responsible rationale asks?
In my dreams – I see myself

Obedience to our own nature. Obedience to the beast.
No beauty to behold. No beauty to but hold. No beauty to unfold. Just another passage of the mind. Told to pass the time as time stands still and we seize our will. The will to power, the faith of a mustard seed. Conjuration and actualization, the ripe fruit of visualization, manifestations of man's infestation. And man's infinite infancy. Infantile in fanatical fascination with the fascism and incredible credos of a nation. Not Zion, new zealots in and on new kicks to tear apart that which makes them sick. Sycophants they have succumbed to living in the umbra of their own brashness. Rash and less than they are wont to be.

Where is that hardened man that used to linger on my doorstep?

His arms crossed in front of him. His eyes glaring out at the world before him. The keeper of my sanctuary. Since when did he lose sight of his job?

How did he ever let anyone in, or anything out?

Where are his callous hands that kept all pain out, and all pain in? Maybe when he turned one day to open that door and look inside. To see what no on was allowed to see, not even him. Maybe he saw the young boy sitting in the middle of that empty room with crossed legs on the hardwood floor. His blackened face peering up towards the opened door at the strong man now scared weak. The boy's charcoal hands, resting lightly on his knees, slowly raise to greet the intruder showing his anorexic ribs covered in soot. Then maybe he ran leaving the door open while the strong eyes of the young boy watched the door.

He yearned for someone to come through and comfort him.

To wash away the blackness and to feed his starving belly. But who can see such a monster and not flee in fear?

Who in their right mind would soil their hands?

Imagine life as an adolescent fitting in with everyone while your mind has been raped into adulthood and your body is beginning the first stages of puberty. Imagine lower class living scrounging for clothes from dumpsters and food stamps to feed yourself on. A seven dollar haircut becomes a luxury as your mother pulls out the scissors and a comb. Popularity is on the opposite pole of your life as time and time again the world teaches you of its ways.

Pleasure to the mind, body and eye is the motive for the motion of the world.

Sex becomes pleasurable only with the beautiful.
Love based on the economy of the individual.
The qualities people look for are dictated by a society that is more unstable than fusion.

A chaotic race – the human race,

spewing forth their kind into a world unwilling to receive. Adapting not ourselves to our environment but our environment to ourselves we destroy the world for which we fight. The hypocrisy of the moment is lost in hindsight as people pleasure their senses with their beauty and their accomplishments pushing the fearful dust of our transgressions under our place-mats. My mind lost in the shuffle, cobwebs forming mixed thoughts and confusion. Contradiction of self in attempt to find thine own self amongst the rubble of a bandwagon society.

The blackness is so ripe.

So many stories to be lost in its color. So dismal blue projected across the room as I sit and try to be anything but me for a minute. Let me be anything any color shape or size, just not me. Let me sink into the music. Let me become twists of sound as a droplet of water churning through empty caverns or soft gentle faeries flying gently through wet leaves. I can almost see just how green they are even though I open my eyes and see to my demise me. I look in a mirror not once, but twice, because how do I know that's really me? I've judged men on less, I've seen wrinkles and explained years of pain as if I had shed those tears through his years. I say those working hands are just slack and coarse but didn't they tie tight bundles of hay and throw mightily underneath a golden sun tanning and breaking the skin of bare working backs. And I've called slut and whore and fake and unlike me – yet it is I who am most unlike me. My face changes as easily as the wind yet I say it is he who is in chains. He who smiles everyday. And oh what chains to be in. Please entrap me. Take away me from wallowing in my own pitiful misery. I judge who I see as I pass by idly as if it were my choice. I judge who I see in the reflection of silver yea he rarely doth pass. He passes judgment and I can stop him not. He is in turmoil and I say he is free. Conflicted as if afflicted but no affliction aside from wandering judging eyes that know not themselves. Sleep I must beg from myself because in my own mind I restlessly stir but why? Isn't that always the question and why do I always question? Can I not break for silence for a moment. Can I not lay to rest without questioning if it's okay? Can I stop dreaming for a moment. Can I stop believing that I am something I am not? But who – what – where am I? Do I know? No, I know not. No negatives or to know negatives because does the mind really comprehend no? Because if no, then why? Why do we ask why to know? I don't know and that's all I have ever known. I become broken in the questions because no matter what I know it's nothing, and of nothing is merely dreams, and in dreams I am nothing but what I dream. But dreams are nothing so I am nothing, I dream of nothing, and become nothing - but nothing has really changed. I am again the faces that I have thus watched change, and again I ask why? Twist my head in circles I know not, my own fate. But pray, I ask, tell me right. Tell me truth. Of all I could ask for in the world, I ask myself to no longer lie to myself. I know not how this to do. Am I really just a pervert with an ache to fill because behind my eyes I ask for truth and naked sex exudes woman's flesh. But I hate the flesh for its monotony in this moment. For its shortcomings. For its wrinkling because it has not transcended time but because its merely stuck in clusters of moments called life. And many clusters of life. What do we call that?

An orgy? No just civilization. Religions like the idea of orgiastic participants and ridiculed laziness of mind. Yet I remember I am not the judge just the vessel of drudgery. In these moments of ineptness that I'm quite experiencing now I find myself dragging down everything into the pit of my mind. But I just know my existential narcissism is what truly believes that everything can be brought down. I begin to wonder if I can change anything and if I can should I try to change it because what if my idea is wrong – I know not truth. I barely know myself none the less anything else.

There is no time, no deeds only reaction to action. One action begins to set upon a course. Reverberating through sanity off the walls of society placed in the mind by repetition then forgetting. When what is forgot becomes forgotten we don't remember but see anew what was once freshly begun and the path can change. A wrinkle can turn or be wiped clean. A brow can raise or fall it would all be the same but societies deeds of time and ill temperament would be lost in the shuffle no longer standing as the dry cobwebs catching the flies of our intuitional imagination before manifested as thought into the subjective universe and thus physically manifested in physical form not just as the optical illusions of eyes wide open daydreaming of things there that aren't. The front joins to the back and the left juxtaposed with the right forming prisms of rainbow color taking the form of grey shades on green, red, blue, and yellow. White and black only exists in the forgotten. To form a thought one must know a hundred things and forget ninety-nine. When one realizes that whatever it knows is nothing remembered only forgotten then it knows nothing for everything changes as time goes on. Yet time exists only in space but not in truth. Truth knows not time because truth does not change. True truth is always true and when contradicted its reverse is destroyed in the forgotten.

To know oneself is a pain of the hardest breed to bear. Bare all to yourself and you will truly know what it is to suffer. Because one must accept one's self at all times. But to know one's self is to know the evil that all men do and then how could you truly judge your neighbor for you have your own slights of mind. In your lust you have wronged, in your life you have sinned. In your eyes you have seen the pain you have caused, the tears you have shed, the blood you have bled. You know it was you who wrongly threw stones. It was you who sang deceitful songs to your lovers. But your lovers know not your heart only the masks that are now falling apart in your introspective melancholic loneliness. Look deeper to find that time has not changed what is always in your heart. Only you can take and learn from your every part. Only you can learn the lessons taught in your life to you, by you, for you. We all have something to learn, and something to earn, for hard work pays off in the end. Look again I ask and plead because,
of all the things I think I know,
I know I don't know me.

Do you ever wonder what its like to be all alone when you are alone?

To understand that ache you feel because you know someone,
something is missing? You contemplate for hours while staring at the
moving air in front of you.
How still your body remains while the gears of your mind restlessly stir
and churn moving you through the past, into and beyond the future.
Wondering if maybe "this is the core of my life". Wondering why you
do it to yourself. The phone a few paces away idle in its place.
You can almost hear the gentle whir of its electric current in the
absence of it ringing. Faintly in your ear you imagine laughter coming
across the line in mid conversation. Dimly daydreaming of those
things that can fill the voids inside.
You may even wonder where that one person is. The person who you
have let become the focal point in your life. A new world established
from co-dependent bonds. Solitude, a word to often used in your
vocabulary, comes to mind as the perfect adjective of your humble
existence.

You find yourself, again, wishing of things.

Hoping that the tension of this (and every other) day can be loosened
by your tongue in flight to a caring, yearning ear.
Your lips stay sealed and tongue taught against the roof of your mouth
as yet another hour of silence passes.
No one hears your thoughts as they strain inward out feeling like a
gushing well trapped beneath your skin.
Your muscles tighten from the strain within and you feel your hands
clutching too tightly against themselves turning the knuckles a hard
bristled white.
Then you remember the empty void inside and the well pumps its wrath
into it drowning nothing with nothing until your body lies still and
empty again.
Your empty eyes stare blankly forward unblinking with a callous
defiance of life but no energy to defy.
You hear your heartbeat in your wrists and feel it clenched in your
teeth. Your marrow seeps your pain into your bloodstream but still no
outlet remains and
solitude becomes your friend.

I have lived many lives.
I've told many tales.
I've crossed time.
I've seen man's heart.
I've touched man's soul.
I've seen many worlds and traveled many places.
I've wept with the dying, cried with heartbreak and pain.
I've traveled lonely roads.
I've smiled at the rain.
I've smelt the ocean's wind and cradled it in my arms.
I've tasted a virgin before any other man.
I've lost my virginity to not one but many.
My heart has been torn and put back together again.
I have loved,
      I have sinned,
            I have lied,
                  I have died.
I have been who I am and I have been hundreds of souls.
Each one less real then the next.
Each one forming the me in my mind.
I have lost myself in worlds beyond compare only to open my eyes and
see pages before me.
Pages that I long to be in.
Pages that trap me.
Pages that I read and want to write.
Tears crash on the pages as smiles follow throughout.

        I only wish to be lost in the pages.
                I only wish to be lost.

What happens now as the lost emotion consumes you to the sound of the music that moves you the most and to the drugs that course through your bloodstream with a mind of their own? You get a little lost and as you stumble in the dark you fall a few times scraping your knees as your needs become figments of some distant awe inspiring imagination that only conceivably was yours in some distant time too far back to remember. It's the amnesia of the soul as the heart grows cold. You write as if you remember truth although you know that this is really all just a dream. But you wonder why you haven't woken up. You can't remember the last time you were really awake and oddly enough, as it were, that fact doesn't bother you. Who wants to be awake for all that shit to deal with. Let me dream in the arms of my lover for I like it there best. Or if that alternative remains unseen then let it be in the drugs we dream. Money becomes no object and no objections to throwing it down our throat or up our nose or sliding it under our tongue. Delirium has an acidic taste that reminds me of a sugar grain. No pain as the smell of cocaine is thrust under my hungrily sniffing nose, and no one knows just how it feels to me and that is what sometimes makes me feel free. Yet – alone. When a world is constructed all for me by me in my head then I am always the only one there. No one else knows the path or the password. No one else sees the beauty. This is insanity and I care not as drowned in the lost emotion my hungry soul begins feeding on itself. Not knowing its own pain it devours itself until things can never be the same again as they were. Not that this is wrong, this is merely my song. The harmony or rather discordant harmony that I symphonize with myself. Rambling never felt so good as it does on overdrive in one-helluva-ransacked mind that I call mine own. Someone once told me that they couldn't be in my life because of drugs because they didn't want to deal with that kind of environment. They were right on the first count but the second, simply mistaken, they can't join me because this my friend is a solitary task. Solitary monotony of vulgar vulgarity. I like the way that sounds almost as if I actually knew what I was talking about. I do that a lot, sound like I know what I'm talking about. I do have a taste of the gift of gab. I just feel bad for those who love me. Can't they see my selfish self-destruction. Don't they realize that even though I can appreciate beauty, life and all things in life, that it really doesn't make a difference in the end because I can't, don't, wont appreciate my own waste of skin? So I'll express it again, I'm lost, and I'm not looking for a way out, I'm looking for a way in.

Freedom -

Who knows the meaning of such a word? So vast its understanding.
The depths to which its fingers tentatively reach as we lie in rest or lie
in deeds. No man heeds freedom's loss for all men already act lost, free
or not.
But what of freedom? What does it really mean?
The loss of a cage?
The loss of age?
The loss of chains?
Or is it only in the mind?
Freedom is what I strive to find. In hindsight freedom can be seen. It
is the gleam of headlights breaking darkness in half across that two lane
highway to nowhere. A broken yellow never ending strip of paint that
leads into tomorrow the lost souls of today. Maybe two tracks, three
feet apart, that metal darts across, locked in place.
Never mistaken is that sound, nor the sound of its whistle blown.
A warning or a farewell.
In its absence, the echo of a conductor's bell. No ticket to ride, no place
to hide. The cities, the mountains, those I call home. Home is where I
sit and where I stand. It is the land beneath me harvested by hands that
slave through another tomorrow. They know not sorrow only silence
for in silence we are all alone and
solitude really is our only true home.
Let me hang my hat. Let me reminisce of my deeds. Let me flee no
more from fate's door. Let me enter into and bask upon my own life for
I can live no other. No bother.
I am me and I live my life.
The only strife is in deeds upon which I strive to live others lives. I
only wish to live my life from this day forth.
To remember my name through the games.
                    To see what it is I am going to see –
                                        That is to live free

In walks the sunshine
and sits at the table
as it props its feet up
on the seat of the chair.

In walks the sunshine
basking in the warmth
of its own light.
Out walks the sunshine.
In walks the night.

Look at the beautiful bodies.
Long to touch their flesh.
A pile of bones lie underneath,
dry withered and disregarded.

Smile at the beautiful bodies.
Lie as you touch their flesh.
The pile of bones stir underneath,
cold, alone, and forgotten.

Close your eyes at the beautiful bodies.
Dirty them as you touch their flesh.
The pile of bones turn to dust,
shallow weak and destroyed.

Forget the beautiful bodies,
deflowered by your flesh.
The pile of dust blows away in the wind,
gone, away, and lost.

Another is born in their place.
Another is destroyed, not with grace.
This is the game that can't be won.
Why does this seem fun?

Money makes the world go round. Lust and looks make hearts pound.
Pleasure is only skin deep. Love is something not to seek. Tears are
begotten of the weak. Fears are begotten of the meek. Strength and
power make a man. Women want money in hand. A beautiful body,
such a delight. A beautiful mind such a ghastly sight. Who wants to
hear "I love you"? Everyone wants to hear, "I'll pay for you". It's no
longer "what can I do to help?" It's only, "how can I help myself?"
Survival of the fittest in a man's world is played with wide open legs of
a girl. Sex, money and power thrive.

How can a man like me ever survive?

Waiting for misery.

For soulless revelations in external relations.

Eye   to   Eye

no deeper than the flesh.

Hand   to   Hand

an eternal three feet away.

What fingers that have caressed now restlessly tap on lonely knees.
Legs crossed in despair.
But no pair thus remains where a union has been held on words of
endearment.
Three words that hurt more now then pleasure evoked afore.
Now silence plays its dominant role of solitude in mixed society.
My eyes see too much and open more doors then listless hands can
close.
The hard splintered oak of which stabs sharply the center there of.

I can only wash the crimson away with bountiful tears.

Click -

Now there is only silence and darkness but the silence is not as quiet as one might originally think. The sounds we normally have forgotten still riddle the night air until we hear them again. They will not stay away they must be heard. They need the same recognition that our soul strives for as it releases its energy into hand, and pen, and page. And we dig deep down into the heart of ourselves and we feel the essence of our organism breathing and beating and trembling much to its own accord and we feel it there, the discordant tremble that things are awry and even still we shall not let our self cry. Tears will not fall from these eyes. We've seen too many lies and like the silence of night that is so loud we have dulled ourselves to the spikes on the ends of so many lovers' tongues and we only brace ourselves for what comes next. Almost like a game show where the next contestant is called on down and we only wonder how long the game will last before the contestant folds, lies and moves on to another game. It's seemingly all about the stakes, what's at stake, who's at stake, what can be won for self. I've almost forgotten that philosophy is a much better place to stand then capitalistic ideology. Capitalizing being, taking advantage of given circumstances or opportunities. But now in the New America its not circumstances that we are taking advantage of, it's one another. It's the fallacy that amuses me, sure I know that a weak man 'tis I. But believe you me, the truth hurts much less then the lie for at least one can still look me in the eye. But now my eyes, as many times before, reminiscing, look into the darkness of the night not hearing its silence and not hearing its noise. Look not into any others eyes for they have hid in shame for they know they lied and they try to forget about me. Still, I can only remember her kiss. Our first kiss the one that brought us to this. Brought us together and then apart. Her to another time, another man, another game. Me to my pen, the only true friend who never forsakes me, who only speaks truth to me even sometimes when I don't want to hear it. Its the friend that tells me of its dreams or sometimes just a whimsical story to make me feel better and sometimes a fantasy to remind me why I live. Sometimes my pen sings me a song, writes me a poem, draws me a picture or just sits and talks about nothing with me. My friend the pen doesn't always make sense but it always tries and is always willing to elaborate. It is there with me no matter my faults, no matter my mood, no matter how much I scream or yell or cry. I can tell it anything and it listens and tells me how it feels. It lets me get everything out so that I can learn how to move on and how to let go of what hurts me so. My friend the pen is with me any day, and everyday I want it close no matter if the sun is shining or it's night. No matter if it's raining or on the odd hours of the day. It doesn't mind if I haven't called in a day, a week, a month or even years. It still comes back to lend me its ears. And even though my friend makes mistakes it's always quick to correct them and never has to apologize because we understand that these things happen. And when all is said and done me and my friend go our separate ways knowing that some day we will be reunited and things will be as they always are, perfectly understood.

Look around at all the empty voids left behind by time and loves erosion. Fill them with what you will, but empty inside you will remain. Burn deep inside with desire like the candle-flame that scars. Feel the walls encroaching you into a dominion unlike any other. Close off the river of emotion, lick the night air with flame's tongue and taste the seclusion of every atomic piece of matter. Explode from inside out as frostbite takes its toll on listless limbs. Use the six senses that hurt the most and revel in the miserly destruction of societies morality as your body partakes of yet another sin. Enjoy liberation in free will where responsibility is based on rosy perspectives. The glasses of deception that dangle from our noses hueing life a pastel grey. A veil of forgetful interpretation. An onslaught of melancholic regurgitation. A rejuvenation of "the" lost emotion. Agitated aggression of comprehensive comprehension mixed with apprehensive apprehension. A colorful prismatic emotional upheaval of the most carnal nature. Creation now a metaphorical science of perspective loneliness. Pain becomes a sign of the times. Our principal, our king is seclusion in solitary monotony of vulgar vulgarity. Language, a new source of frustration, an outlet for societies charms, becomes what we do and not how we say what we say when we think what we cannot think.

Thoughts the new void of pale pitch black.

What we think, we become.
What we become, we animate.
What we animate, we destroy.

It is the ultimate narcissistic self destruct method practiced by lonely man.

Rivers of emotions
that pour from our souls create a delta.
Our boat
paddles up the current
of each branch slowly,
sluggish.
An eddying flow.
Narcissism becomes the undertow
as time and time again our boat flips
and we
are washed out to sea merely to crawl back in for another go.
Ego
is the typhoon
that whips
the shawl
from your
shoulders
and the
hat
from my head.
The whirlwind crashing the cold rain against our naked flesh.
Vanity
is the piranhas that jump from the murky water to nibble at our skin and
strip us of our necessities.
Love
is the sunshine that warms our skin after bitter struggle with forces not
in our control.

I have never once proven myself to her.
Only many times over dashed her hopes against the jagged shores of
abandon-less love. Silence shall be my vestibule and an observer once
again shall I become.
                    The world I live in shall live on the page.
My mind merely an unfocused vortex spewing forth thought and
emotion into the mainstream of unidealistic dreams.
                    A facade of faces and masks.
The eyes shadowed and mirrored towards the ways of a true society
that hides itself within its system of hypocrisy, lies, games and failures.
            Happiness is being content and content I am not.
Filled with contempt for a world whose half face of ugly distraught has
been thrust before my eyes without me beseeching it as such.
Coarseness of lessons cause legions and callouses upon an already
charred heart. You find the solution to an ever changing puzzle, pitfalls
and traps lining your path to mystical freedom in someone else's arms.
A mythical dream where the sun revolves around you;
                    an entity in and of itself.
Perplexing pandemonium, an apocalypse of sanity into its purest form.
Life's acid trip of a joke. A kaleidoscope of hope. Shimmering then
changing before your eyes. Laughing, joking, taunting you to play its
game by its constant changing rules.
                    Who are you to play?

Tonight I can see the games but cannot play. For every inch of my
strength pours into holding onto what little I have left of a grasp on
things. Yet I realize these games that everyone is lost in is necessary to
life in and of itself. At least in some ways. I sit here almost
expressionless, barely able to even greet those passing by as they play
and I realize what a vital role this game is.
                    It is my every expression.
                My every whim or fleeting glance.
                    It is why I dance.
And I want to scream from the inside out because although I hate to
play, I almost have to believe that I have no choice but
                    to play or to die.

I move this book so gently between my hands almost as if had I not, some words would have fallen out and been lost or misplaced.
In the silence – silence is almost confusing.
And when you say every last word you can to hopefully sway my way, I smile inside because I trust you; that you do it to help and not harm.

And you across the way-
Do you see me watching you as you preen and pose?
Your moves so exacting no other truth could be told.
The extra eyes that perch upon my drawn little finger watch and remember for me the deeds of this night as it takes flight just to come crashing down again.
Those little things you do when you forget and think that no one is watching,

I see,
and I like to watch,
because they tell to me more things then your agape breathing mouth could ever say.
How many of you are as fascinated by me in my deeds as I am of you in yours? Sometimes you catch me looking and it makes you wonder I know.

It makes you question.
Go ahead and make your motions, your gestures because you know I'm watching. Do what you do best because I'll be following shortly thereafter with my eyelashes batting not away a single beat from the music you play as you try to lay out your symphony for me to play my instrument upon. Each of my instruments pounding away at the tempo you have created. But you knew not the number nor the decibel of my manifold instruments and upon your seemingly harmonious symphony my instruments explode with music so deafening it engulfs you and eventually engulfs me
drowning us in

the music you wrote,
I played to,
and ironically,
we both died in.

Be not deceived by my playing hands and idle eyes.
I am no fool amidst a team of wolves.
Hungry and thirsty,

                    hunting
                       in
                    parade
                    fashion
These slow moving eyes have seen enough.
The games, the lies that fuel the hunt. If it be my ignorance in question
then your trick has already failed for I have seen and I have controlled
what I have displayed. No matter the mask adorned my eyes still
unscathed,

        unblinded   unblinking
                      remain

    The fallacy but a vessel to be shipwrecked on my shores.
    As the fog light of your self realization is lost in the smog.

                              I am but what you make of me.

31

Do you remember small time suburbia playing in the mud and wondering a tree's shape as the sun cracked through the leaves to shine and bake mud pies caked to your hands? Your shirtless body, sock-less feet and already stained brown, blue jeans that your mother swore "you better not get dirty, they cost me three dollars." But of course we just hoped for a penny to be found in the afterlife of a pocket with a hole from any man's clean trousers so we could get a gumball to stick in our sisters hair after we chewed it and she hit us in the arm because she wanted one too. We don't mind sharing we think to ourselves as long as we have more than one. In the drama of her tongue we forgot a green, lonely swimming frog, upside down now, in a bucket of water. A pot mom wasn't using to cook the rice we will be having for dinner and lunch and dinner yesterday and tomorrow. Now we wouldn't have that pet like we oh so wanted so bad, not that our mother would let us keep it. And then in a fit of childish depression we want to run and hide but not in a hole. We want to soar higher out of the rut seemingly trapping us in a moment we have not designed. My fingers dig into the bark of that tree that the sun cracked through and my legs grab tight the trunk as I claw and clutch up that tree reaching for the shortest limb to hold my eighty pounds of weight off of the muddy trampled ground soaked from a green water hose we left running. But then up there the breeze attacks our face with a soothing comforting embrace and as a child all becomes forget in our heart and all we know is the freedom felt in the scratches and cuts in our arms and legs from scaling thirty feet into the air being that much closer to the beautiful warm ball floating slowly across the sky. We try to forget the time we have to return to the inside world behind those walls where there are so many rules. Just because that beautiful ball falls every night do we have to come in? But we refrain from a temper tantrum 'cause we don't find a bad temperament fun. So we forget all that and stare at the day loving the moment. Just that moment and no other because we knew then it wouldn't last. That it would change and we would have to change with it because that's just how it is. Instead of fighting for what we know cannot be. Why must the day be what we want it? Why can't it be what it is and with it we be satisfied? As we were as a child. A child basking in the warmth of this moment. We seem to be more free when we are free in our mind to change. Time and this moment will change. As a child we walked with the moment and now we almost try to make the moment. I want the child in me to become the me I already am to learn again how to be free.

If you could be anything just what would you be? If you saw yourself as that thing just what would you be doing? Would you be hitting that pipe and asking for more or would you be running for the door? Would you wake up in the morning with a crimson nose a flood or would you jog two miles all with a smile, feeling oh so good? Lungs filling with air so fresh; never out of breath from one flight of stairs; no cares in the world at all. Me, I'd be free, free to do anything that I want; to live as I see best. "How is that?" one might ask, yet answering that is the hard task. Do you really know how you should live until you die and get the answer to the ever elusive question why? I say to myself never fear, never cry, just live your life. Walk down the path and learn of yourself all you can ever do is your best, forget the rest. Mistakes and questions, it's all just a game, remember your name and who you are. Just what you have to say for that is the way to live. Life is a sacrifice and in it we must give. Receiving is not an option, believing just a perspective. Too many facets for any one man to track. That is why we all have our own paths. You see, I'm not an artist, not a poet, not a man, just a boy of the world trying to understand. To live, experience, express and learn, it has nothing to do with the dollars that we earn. I could care less about the green if you know what I mean. I just want to get where I'm going.

A dark shadowy silhouette stands silently beneath the blackened leafless ash tree that stands beneath a foreshadowing sky of mixed grey hues and lifeless voids. The wind stirs grotesquely through damp mildewed leaves and not one living creature nor thing moves as time stands still. Two white spots amongst that picture of bleak shine mistily centered near the top of the round head of the shadowy silhouette. Slowly, only one breath at a time the silent silhouette of shadows revolves until the pale white orbs can be seen no more. Opaqueness of black to translucent grey the shadowy silhouette transforms into what appears to be just another dream.

A wakeful euphoric state of the conscious subconscious. An insight into darkness. Voids full of promising answers. Looking with the magnifying glass of child like perception. The mind a sponge for knowledge as the rest of the body lies still eyes unblinking no need to hide only perceive without deception for no masks are invisible in this moment.

How can silence be so loud? Its deafening roar an incessant pounding in my ears. Like music, its tempo and rhythm fill you from the soul out tempting you to break in with a foreign beat. Silence talks to me of more things than a thousand words. Even stronger silence is, when the sun cannot be seen behind miles of grey and white clouds. The wind's fingers brush across my face sealing my lips. The only free piece of humanity in me is my thoughts although they too are tainted. Pain can be most easily remembered in silence and most easily felt in the absence therein. There is no laughter in silence only tight-lipped smiles. My face a contortion of the pain remembered. My expressions a book into my life where the pages are written in callous wrinkles with time's quill pen.

A soft night breeze with the scent of rain pulls gently at the candlelight which flickers through glassy eyes. The sky dark and shadowed with invisible clouds that gently fall to the earth with a soothing mother-like tempo. Your face inches away from the pages feels the heat of a strawberry perfumed candle. The red light merely a whisper across the page feeding your eyes just enough to see. Green leaves droop in slumber as roots drink hungrily at the rain. The ground soaking in the sky's misery as the moon charts a path into tomorrow's sun rise. The lights of many houses burn still in the wee hours of midnight gone. Crickets and locust break the dead silence of night singing to their mates in an abandon-less search for companionship and meaning. The black curtain of night pulls heavy on your eyelids and sleep tempts you with its wishful dreams and oh too often your hands stray from your pen in search of another. Or in search of a pillow to nestle your ear upon to hide your tears 'til replaced by morning's glory.

Define suffering.

Is it the ache you feel in your stomach when it's been ten hours since you last ate? Is it the sting you feel from cracked bones? Or maybe it's just the emptiness inside that we all long to fill. Maybe when you are all alone and you have those ten hours to sit and think about your life to wonder where the future is headed and how fast you are going to get there. Maybe it's the scream you hold inside that begs to be released into black silence. The candles that feed you light. The night air the only thing holding you tight when all of you is straining to get out. A fire's burning wrath against your strong forearm. Childhood memories of laughter and scorn at you. Narcissism, the world revolving around you. But doesn't it? Who else is in this world but you. Who else feels you? Who lives your life? Aren't we all really alone? No one is inside me. I won't even let me in. What is this world of politics, religion, sex and money? What are the clouds really saying? What does the rain wash away that a flood of tears can't touch? What is pain other then a memory? What is a memoir? Is it that thought you had yesterday or maybe just that paper-cut from junior high. Maybe just those things that toss and turn you at night covered beneath those blankets. What is light? Is it the absence of darkness or just that figure you saw beside your bed when you were seven.

Define life.

Is it that ache you feel in your stomach when it's been ten hours since you last ate? Or just the sting you feel in cracked bones. Maybe it's the air you can't stand to breath. Maybe its that scream. What about the sunshine? Where does it lead except into night. Where does the moon lead except into melancholic loneliness. Where does this year take you but into your next memoir.

Define suffering.

Maybe it's nothing at all. Maybe it's you.

How long can you run? How far away before the pain is gone? Where must you hide? Looking over that lonely shoulder that thousands of tears were shed on, now shedding fresh tears in place of dryly forgotten aches. How long can you sabotage your life with ill placed indecisiveness? Freedom does not exist in a mind plagued with thoughts, fears, and emotions. The world says stop when you're screaming go and just in the middle of rush hour you can't slow down the turning wheels of life's game played by forces so inconceivably inevitable. You long for sleep when you awake. You long for sleep as you lay awake at night filled with terror. You long for the day in your dreams. Beseeching freedom, your soul screams. No one hears its voice as you feel your pain. There is no escape. No dismissal of dismal fate.

I see that blue light shining on the road tempting me to walk its path into the darkness beyond. Still I sit behind the comforting light of burning candles. The horizon can never be touched no matter how much we long. Every step closer pushes it one step farther away. No matter how far out you stretch your feeble arms, you can never touch the sacred place at the end of the rainbow. The colors of which burn painful memories into your retinas. Draw from another cigarette the comforting pain of realizing reality.

Deep inside me there is a beast.
With red glowing eyes and sharp teeth.
A ferocious bite the beast displays.
Claws extended, ripping in the middle of fray.

Its bridle snaps with the twist of its neck.
The muscles of its back churn in a growl.
Its legs taught ready to spring forth from my bosom.
The drool from its lip disgusting and foul.

Wretched misery, the black stone of its heart.
Seething anger, the gleam in its eye.
Callous pain and frustration, the silvery claws.
Pain, the outstanding fuel for its cause.

What has become of my emotions
as life has defiled and berated them?
Such an ugly thing that hideth beneath my bed.
That hideth in my soul pretending to be dead.
True death of the beast comes from
the true arrow of soulful love.
Drum-drum, beat-beat, drum-drum
The heart of the beast is idle but strong.

There once was a man whom emotions consumed overflowing with warmth, vitality and life despite the murky waters of a life less desirable. Then lost love entered his mind and now he may not lay to rest, for the nature of the beast within that encompasses his heart with charred hands and razor sharp teeth that dig into that pumping vessel. Too often the cheapness of a moment is procured by the hindsight of an evil vixen. Never a warm eye held in an embracing stare shall once again reign where tremors of the heart have been stifled by such idle hands and lazy tongues beseeching another's mouth. The moon but a reminder of the distance of peace. How far away from a lonely yearning grasp it doth stray in the middle of yet another lonely night. Freedom for my soul is but death in my heart. The beheading of my emotions. The capture of the lost emotion. Tranquility is death's glassy eyed stare at the emotional upheaval of the world thus proclaimed. Destruction of the primal forces of nature leave me empty inside once again.

A man sitting in the middle of the wall of an almost empty living room listening to music also adorned on the ears of a sleeping woman sprawled on a broken couch, lifted end by books or broken pegs. His arms resting hard on knees spread at an angle precariously to dangle his head between two hands. Empty was one, cigarette burning fingers in the other as smoke curls and wafts through the still air of the afternoon's musky room. The pet, a grey cat, only kind enough to trap his lap and arms with gentle purrs and soft loving whispers when the time is not right. Nibbling at arms linked to hands that do not pet because tired in the heart a lonely man who hath slept all day to kiss the day away before the night could be vanquished in the song of no new lovers. No lovers at all. With no arms embracing tight upon another. A tipped stool white legs brown round top lays under a heavily burdened coat rack from half a dozen coats not worn by half a dozen people not here nor there. Nor anywhere in sight or arms length. Discarded boots black and empty from sock clad feet trudging through the day of another week. Another work day to feed hungry mouths not fed in days except by limp noodles boiled in brown broth and served with steaming heat too warm to taste on charred tongues. Black blank TV screen once mused over as multiple images projected across entertained idle minds wasting the time of days not worked nor played. Idle guitar strings from white porcelain machine strummed not by fingers idly plucking noise into the quiet day riddled with noisy revs of traffic cars and bikes glistening in sunshine not seen by eyes hid in four walls and green carpets blackened by feet treading the dirt of the outside world into the inside world lit only by blue and orange fluorescent and fake light pale and homely like white skin not tanned from the sunny beach or warm glistening water poolside in summer's heat for winter's cold has seized the fumes of a city big enough to get lost in, small enough to remain forgotten. A siren singing before another engine revved as the final destination is dispatched over a loud black box muffled in the crackle of static voices sticking to the ears of career men and women saving and destroying lives amidst the wolves of society. Two decks of cards discarded on brown mantles waiting to join in the game of interaction between two or more hands. Cigarettes lit smoked, forgotten, lights another with a smoky reside to leave an empty brown potch-marked filter dirty and lonely joined by others to fill the void of melancholy in an almost empty black cigarette graveyard. A tray of ashes, a coffin for the forgotten. An after life for the once lived, once smoked, spark of tobacco brown and now filmy on the lungs of millions to come and go in their own coffin. Books lonely cover to cover, not read, sit silently in repose holding in the knowledge of their text before opened, before read then discarded for another's soft papyrus texture endearing hazel eyes changing green or brown like fall leaves to orange and red. Look not at the conifers or counterfeits - always green. No matter the color, blue or white, of precipitation, warm or cold or bold. The wind also changing from open and trusting to closed and harsh, charging the fuel to use the coats on a brown coat rack standing solitary by itself only accompanied by lazy eyes dreaming while opened wide or closed tight in slumber.

Now lay silently, speaking not a word, on soft cushions protecting the floor from your flesh and your flesh from the floor and listen intently to the silence of the phone as it rings not a discordance upon your ears beseeching answers to questions it has not, nor knows, for days could pass without being asked, without being answered. How lonely could that black box be for it always sits in repose whether answered or not, asked or not, it does not change except when grasped and raised to an ear cold or red with warmth and embarrassment, "Hello? Is anybody there?" - No, not always. The hands of a digital clock point at five and zero and four. Illuminated neon green those hands move so slow into tomorrow. How many hours of silence must pass before forgotten in the next?

Circumnavigate that which cannot be described.
Lost art becomes what we are saying as opposed to what we are really
talking about.
Or have you not yet heard the words?
Have you not yet conjugated the verbs?
Are you wont not of understanding and not understanding that that is
the plan and path of the curved words, twisted and maligned.
Not, dare I say, malignant for such would be transgression on the nature
of that for which the words only have illusive meaning.
Or is it to taste that which is of another's breath.
Speak of soul, one's soul speak.
Formed not in vibration and organic harmonics.
No dance of the pallet could truly describe the contracting fibers
beneath a cornea lying to that which lies well enough alone on its own.

You know how you don't hear a constant sound until it stops?
That's life.
Forgotten in the background of things seemingly more glorious. But what beauty all alone it stands. Its own sun. Its own night. The whole sphere of itself basking in the warmth of itself beginning and end all the same just as time begins to not exist. The motion a current so gentle like waves of music reverberating from tightly drawn copper twisted a thousand times around itself and then plucked one, two, three in rhythm to a foot tapping to fours in groups of two as three stand. Yes, confusing is life. Hard to see the shell from within without slicing through. Without breaking some ice. An electron can be seen only by the path it leaves behind. We are but electrons in the grander scheme of things only no one is holding the magnifying glass looking for our trails.

Empty lots with cracked cement and broken twigs.
Air stirring only in passing.
Cold and dark as it should be.
Dry and withered in the sun.
Barren, desolate, lonely - what difference does it make?
Still and silent it remains even in the absence of flesh.
A graveyard of memories.
That stolen drunken kiss under the starlight. The angry bottle thrown
shattered into green and brown pieces. The musky scent of beer
forgotten as dried in the rain of yesterday under today's dewy sunrise.
The squeal of tires marked black and crimson on pavement charcoal
grey. Bumbling and homeless sleeping in rags from twenty dumpsters
in the back alleys of bars and pubs and homes not seen by daylight's
eye of prosperity and warmth. The blanket of the night sky whispering
fairy tale bedtime stories to cities that sleep. To cities that don't. To
jungles and rivers and crickets with broken wings and doves with
broken hearts. A million scraps of confetti; blue, or red, black or white.
Torn from IRS audits of multi-billionaires who lost in the shuffle a few
p's, q's and dollar signs. Dusty cobwebs, grey and hairy, wafting
slightly from left to right trapped against two red bricked walls.
Another day is born as tomorrow comes.
Where are you when my arms are open, divided down the center?

All the colors and shapes warping through your mind. But what is it worth? What is it worth to you? One paycheck or two. Or a month's sweat to get off just that once. And you try to define a fiend as your mouth opens for another dose of the closest thing to insanity you could ever dream of tasting. You wonder how many hours 'til sunrise? 'Til another day of work begins without me. Until I don my uniform, trudge out into society and smile as I pass every passerby who can't smile because fear of penetration of their own sphere encompasses the black shroud they once called their hearts. And another minute passes to no avail and no more peace from loneliness as yet ten thousand more thoughts plague the mush in your skull asking to be answered. And not with questions because to ask again what we don't want to hear the answer to is just another nail in our coffin which slowly lowers into the dirt grave we call our existence as society takes its toll and another corporate America baby is born in a world of war on CNN and atomic bombs in anyone's bathroom waiting to explode into another year where we fight against all colors not mirrored to our own and beliefs we can't accept because we are always right. Right? WRONG. If you can't see the diversity of mankind locked deeper into your soul than Adam's lost rib, then you are blind to the true nature of yourself. The true nature of a harmonious universe trying to cope with itself – within itself. The world holds what it has in its hands and its nimble fingers play with that clay shaping tomorrow before today has even been born into our minds. But that is the flow of life. All life has a flow, just as my pen on this page. I hold on tight to the flow eddying from the ocean of my mind trying not to lose the flow in the undertow of my environment or the drugs that warp my senses into something like a lackluster dream for heaven when the hell we all created becomes our existence. Life is too short, so we get off before we get on trying to hold onto what's left of our lives as we see the end ever pressing forward trying to oppress the energy that keeps us striving on even when it hurts deep down in the gut of your stomach and almost makes you want to double over. Puke. Let out the wretched taste of society because they don't understand the universality of the loner. The man who stands alone. Not because he can't function in the games and masks that take harbor on all faces but because he knows that the masks are just that. Foolish toys for the children who don't know better because they are raised as sheep. But who am I to look and judge as rock, rock, another hour passes in this velvet orange rocking chair that holds a man whose body rocked with drugs doesn't even know if what he's looking at is really there at all. Is anything really there? That smoke stained carpet or fake fireplace? What about those other lost souls taking harbor in fleshen shells called friends? What about anything, everything, nothing? That is the answer. There is nothing. Nothing really matters. It's all perspective which is why everyone wants to agree on perspectives. Let's see how many we can get in sync with our delusions so that we can call it our own harsh realities. The harsh reality of it all is that nothing has changed. We all want someone close because we can't explain how that ache is cured and hole filled. And does it even matter if we could. We all want to be seen as real because we can't deny our own existence without dying before our time. We all want to enjoy every moment that we can for it's too harsh not to. We all have different paths. Mine lost in drugs and the written words. Maybe yours lost in corporate America where the almighty buck rules your life. Or maybe neither of those. But I'll always prefer to be an artist rather then another one of societies children.

Flashing neon lights swaying to music ripe. Beats pounding like wanton flesh, dripping with sex, exuding sweat. Forgotten tales and memoirs under eyes glazed and rolled back into a head hazed from thought. Another pumping vessel the body becomes mixing with the music the taste of passion on bitter tongues pale with sugar coated kindness and forgotten lore. Slow then speak deep thoughts, no melancholy in turbulence so sweet and provoking. Provocative in dim lights. Curves and circles to fill the pallet of the mind's colors. So rare doth these hands move with such a fervent rhythm. Harmonious only to the papyrus they destroy in marks of passion. Hours of silence may pass or all noise filled smoke clouded filled body rooms charged and pumped torn and thrust forever moving and changing interacting from beat to beat moment to moment only another lost in tomorrow or today but who cares anyways. A twisty road with broken city skyline grey omnipresent foreshadowing or just long shadows as the sun slowly falls from the sky. But what of the oceans and orange hued dusky deserts with mounds of dunes piling up grain by grain into a breathtaking landscape. Confused, bewildered. Merely lost in the shuffle. Too much to track a thousand patterns of the stars on the moon or the moon is just the sun's devil's advocate trapped in its own existence not able to see its own reflection. Not able to gaze upon its glorious beauty so far from the mirror of the placid lake locked in chains of a mountain guarding the fertile land and tall growing trees. But not free those leaves do not fall but merely raise the dead twigs of trees bare in winter's sorrow or summer's tomorrow. How many times may one forget to exist? One life is provoked by many but lived by one once and no more until another form of life is begot from being sought. From being found. Created from two mingling reacting and acting against yet for one another into one that multiplies into many by joining the juxtaposition of millions into one. But no interaction thus founded is confined within such shells of disharmony. Such shells entrapping the life giving force of eternity. No more time exists in this space. But in this time there is space until we all have traveled far beyond our own flesh ridden limitations beyond the cosmos into what becomes tomorrow, a moment not like this or any other. No bother. No stopping the flow from life to life as interaction to interaction fuels, feeds, forces unto another sun another moon to mirror its glorious light. To spread that light to share with the milky tapped waves rolling against a darker ocean broad, stripped, and bare of necessities. Sea shells worn ragged and beautiful in the years just as our faces in age. Such beauty to be admired in the changing of the natural into more natural flowing states. Thrown, a stone puddles and ripples through a creek slowing its course until it has come to a final resting place. Then tousled and turned amidst turbulence. Smoother and finer and more finite it grows until it too has been cast out to sea to wash upon shores of castles with rocks majestic and eerie peering over the sea of life. The waves under no moon pull not so tight and finally rest their ears with no more sound of the ocean but finally that of the wind in the trees or the sun on bare working backs. Tired and now resting.

Looking at the room of a crazed tripping man seeing broken cigarettes, four-year old poems on tattered paper adorned precariously in the middle of the floor. A glue stick not used only half a thought formed. Another couple shoe boxes open revealing a younger time of mind more timid and hidden, unaware as it were, maybe as it is. Pens with flipped caps. Cigarette graveyards filled to the brim. Covers thrown aside of the bed with clean laundry keeping the pillows warm. Pornos many times displayed and played hours before now idle on the floor or in the VCR/TV or half in/out of a casing. A cigarette pack three-quarters full and a Zippo smeared with greasy sweat streaked fingerprints. A tape recorder almost impossible to figure out recorded a nice train of thought now silent unlike my current thoughts and still I look and I must say as always – it's been a good night.

The pain burns so hot now that all becomes numb in the mind. Until the floodgate is breached and then released. But the pain is no longer the same, it has changed. It destroys first one part then another of the body, leaving the trails of its passing in scars and bloodshed and eventually death. It is possible to die of a broken heart. I have been dying for years. Knowing this, I've tried to hasten the end to today yet to no avail. All I have done is multiplied my suffering, exhausted my options and hurt others in the process. I have taken my pain and lain it on the shoulders of my neighbors, my peers, my lovers. This is a crime which should bear the penalty of death, yet I live merely judged, merely hoping the sentence could be carried out sooner. I have no qualms about dying. It's the waiting and anticipation that bothers me so. Tell me I shall die and with open arms I'd accept that judgment. But to merely dangle it before my eyes is torture. And so I suffer. I should not cry and wine about such things for there are those who suffer who have committed no crimes. Yet I still wonder why the crimes I have committed carry the wait of this torture I have begun to call my life. Why can I not be delivered from my burdens? Who will save me? Who will be my redeemer? And dare you say God? The same God I loved with my whole heart who let me be raped as a child? The same God who I still love even though my judgment tells me he's not real, nor really there. How am I to see this God when I cannot escape the depths of sin that I have immersed myself neck high in unbeknownst to my childlike mind. Sin found me when I felt I had nothing there for me, no one there for me, and so I embraced it with open arms. I made lust my lover, hate my savior, destruction my livelihood and death my destiny. I walked the path with these vices and destroyed the man that I was and became the beast that I am. Lonely without a friend. And no one wants to hear my tales of plight for they have their own. And all I want now is someone to listen, someone to comfort me and perhaps, if fortune would smile upon me, someone to guide me. Such dreams will not be realized. For this is not a world I created. The demons in life have a hold of me. Their steadfast grip so tight that my own deeds begin to turn my stomach so that all I wish to do is puke. I can never puke or cry enough. It is impossible to reject one's self from one's self. My only fear is that even death will not save me. Perhaps I am too far gone to ever experience true happiness again. There once was a time when I thought I had a chance. Now is not that time. I will sin again, this much I know. And I will die in time. This too is true. Yet will I ever be free? Free from myself and free from the pain of others. I fear the answer is no. If there is a God may he have mercy on my soul.

The only way to get to the end game is to take risks and push your limits. To see the final answer one must be prepared to ask all the questions. Limitations are myths of the mind. Consciousness as we know it is perspective. Consciousness of truth is being. We know not that we are, thus question this, and cannot be as we are – hence philosophy is born. Some care not to question only elucidate what we already think we know – hence poetry is born. Some of us care not to know and thus forget ourselves – hence man is born. Physical limitations are born from the myth that the way of the flesh is being. As we are, we may be in flesh but flesh is not being. I have been as many things and will be as many more. Thus my physical fleshen limitations do not exist. I choose limitations as guidelines for directions only in the sense that they are the stairs I climb to go up or down or the halls I walk to turn left or right but they do not define my being within them. I, as being, define them for proper use in motivation and therefore travel, yet travel as being exists not because my place is always my place and there is no other place then the place that I am being. All other figurative places are within that place and within my being it is my harmony with them that is changed. Either in accord or discord. To know them is in accord. To want for them is discord. To know them is to be them as I already am. There is no fleshen conscious correlation to this feat because to be conscious is to perceive and to perceive is to question how to perceive and in question we cannot know. True faith without question is to know. Thus consciously we cannot enter a state of truth. Perhaps the subconscious and alter-conscious states question not because they only do as if they know as in blind faith. Yet they rely on conscious information which is false information. Thus they believe blindly in false information and thus can never know if what they believe is really truth. Perhaps you'll say that my writing must therefore be false. I write because it is the only way I know how to express myself as I am. Many people are awake and yet not conscious yet also not being in truth. Their consciousness is in a state of blinders as on a horse. They filter out all irrelevant information. The only information allowed into their conscious state is that which will keep them in their loop of conscious comfort. A pain dulling technique if you will. Yet there are those few people with the select gift of being that can enter into being without conscious attention. You may know of them as psychics or priests or incredibly enlightened or the clinically, and I emphasize "socially", insane. The insane as our society describes them are most undoubtedly always in a constant state of being, hence the inability to use the logic conscience people use because they question not. All they know is that; as they are, in being, is truth. Which I agree with, and thus they are in each moment exactly as they are comprised. If they must defecate in a moment then that is as they are and as they are they act as they are and thus defecate regardless of the logical social conscious situation. Appropriate or inappropriate is not a matter of question because they question nothing. They are as they are. This is not to say that being "insane" is ideal. As the beings that we are, we are built to be conscious and thus question and find our paths of being to being. Essentially, form matters not as being for being requires no specific form. Thus essentially we are truly always being as we are although this form is mainly restricted based on the general rules of its structure from being in truth, thus knowing truth. Many people are content in not knowing truth yet. Others hasten to truth as quickly as possible. All beings already know truth, yet not all are in harmony with truth. Thus they are not in harmony with all other things. This drives various beings to search for harmony amongst forms. Thus groups are formed and structures are built. Thus language is born, music is born, religion is born, societies are born and in them the substructures of politics and science. Stereotypes show definition in separate harmonies and thus in stereotypes limitations are born. False fleshen limitations that we believe because we question, because we believe in the structures we have created and because we know. *The greatest and original sin to truth is to know consciously.* The proof is that harmony is a certain matter of acceptance. To accept oneself is to know, in truth, one's self. To question one's self is to presuppose the possibility that one may not be as one is. This is not accepting oneself thus creating anti-harmony or discord. Sin by my definition is to go against that which is pure. Harmony is pure. Discord is impure. Thus knowing consciously – or questioning is to go against harmony, thus that which is pure. Thus, knowing consciously is the highest sin for it tries to negate being in truth. I strive for truth in being in any form for that is my conscious path. That is how I strive for harmony within myself. But make no mistake all beings are on their course and thus as they are (even though as flesh, we are sin) and therefore all are correct or right or in discordant harmony. So, furthermore, that which goes without saying is, I am neither right nor wrong and therefore no better nor lesser than any other being. I merely am as I am and that is all I can ever be.

In back alleys crouched beneath rotted wooden planks for a roof out of the drizzling rain from the bleak grey sky. Little droplets falling so slowly a hand held out catches a thousand tears before they puddle into a river of emotions. Streaming down the sidewalk, down fall, leave ridden gutters next to chipped curbs, yellow paint and telephone poles. Trash strewn city with hidden needles in dumpsters and cracky-sacks worth their weight in gold. Acid, chargers, crackers used. Balloons busted in the freezing cold as the humidity reaches eighty. Callous fingers digging and scratching wayward flesh. No caresses endeared. Nothing feared. No words of modesty from solemn men on corner blocks with Styrofoam cups and tenth generation shawls. Klink-klink thirty-five cents never sounded so good. Another forty empty and discarded. Another sack with water and baking soda smoked from rolled aluminum foil and mangled fingers with broken nails and bile soaked skin the color of jaundice third degree. Six degrees of revolution. But no anarchy. Just a million friends and no one to talk to. No one to listen to the tales. Ink flows so long thinned in rain or tears, or blood, or pain. The three syllable dialect of a child begins to make more sense than the governor's lies. Displayed through pawn shop windows on your neighbor's TV for twenty-five dollars paid to the man on the corner for another dose of gold or silver mercury to course through sterling silver needles into the race-track of crimson and blue. Blue like the lips of that non-breathing form underneath a rock hard blanket. Blanketed in ice from last night's below zero snow storm because the 'whale's tale' was too expensive and nobody left a dime in a topless McDonald's drinking utensil, straw-less and hopeless. No straws left to pull but the short one. No more chances or belated forgiveness so kind. Another blast and a thousand are blind. Famine is the ribs of a hundred children bare. No loin clothes to hide the shame of tattered limbs. Of bones housed in tightly drawn skin of malnourishment. One tooth left. None to gnaw. Rice and pudding cakes smashed and fed through a straw to a throat porous dry and closed to a belly the size of a quarter churning, hungry and empty, not fed. Three trillion dollars of deficit. Four trillion in the bank. A handful of men with the checkbooks and not a care among their ranks. Rank like the smell of defecation from loss of self-control. Ketamine or ketaset we wouldn't tell a soul. Yellow stained or deceived, briefs or teeth, bone or skin, minds hazed with heat. A hundred degrees of summertime, or a hundred pounds of exhaust. The fumes and smog it's a congestion high. One in three miles or a thousand to nine. But whom is really free? Cages of home, chains of work. The economy on the uprise. Do not overthrow, there will be no coup, for one mind is seemingly greater than two. A man or a woman, white or black. The president but one of us; tainted as we are in the gutters by lust and hate, greed and deceit, the lies the games, no man escapes. The blood may boil in a golden chalice broken brown and crusty before touched to parched lips in the desert wasteland of Jerusalem, or Eden, or the Nevada sky line. Twenty on one corner, fifty on the next. Next stop to the county will be thirty-five or the other county life with no chance of parole as twenty-five years served with good behavior sets free another one of us. Killers, or rapists, or child molesters. How were they raised? How long is the victim sentenced for the crime committed? That is always *life*. Every corner sought, every high begot, every memory forgot leaves another black hole in societies mentality sucking another handful in to the other side of life. To the darker side of humanity where junkies and dealers dwell. The spawn of an unforgiving society who has no other cheek to turn because torn under the eyes the black bags hang in a pair more lonely then a man on the moon. Dark shades hang from bleeding noses torn with glass from a pinched sack that was crushed and minced into a fine white powder sharp as diamonds and hot like the ice bursting balloons. Two fingers scarred, palms torn, not able to be read. The life line so short and so many years now his name on the report is merely dead, or John Doe. But what does John do? The same as you and I, he tries to survive. Hold the hands of life. Stumble to the edge. Jagged shores protrude against the black ocean's horizon with the white capped waves of another tsunami. Where were you for Sunday mass or mass hysteria? Riots and flaming cocktails forgot in Martini's dry to the bone. The cosmopolitan man or woman trying to be Neapolitan or Napoleon. If one king remains we are all the thorns in his crown. A crimson river under our feet as our actions walk us down the hall to the principal's office, four years before we make last call at the corner bar with dollar drafts and for another quarter, another shot. A shot of a black house, or another life. Forgotten in intoxication or LSD, K or coke, cake or crack, or that blissful second in another whore's arms whose eyes watch the clock for every second of that hour spent opened in the flesh but closed at the heart. Numb legs thrown up over obese soldiers. Like the numb emotions discarded for a paycheck of survival. Fifteen dollars to blow. Or to blow for fifteen dollars. Fifteen dollars for blow is but a quarter of a teener. Eight more lines to forget cut short and sweet, laxative like, powdery fine as for an Olympic slalom on ice. Hey yo, this isn't Yahtzee, but shake and throw the dice again. The odds must improve you can't crap out twice. Crack out a thousand times for it will never be enough until tight lipped smiles are blue and glued in a frown. What is your outlet? AC or DC, the pen or a friend? Charged with the voltage we all carry. No ohms to resist. No alms to assist. Copper wire or pennies, Nickel Cadmium soaked. The chains of gold taut and tight, the fingers of fright. Fear a year and it may be your last. A day no way we must survive for we haven't gotten enough high. The tabloids dictating fashion and feeding the mind of lies. Is figer-after-the-Hil really your best thrill? Or should we play polo with collars turned up like fake smiles revealing fake gold plated teeth, wooden in our skulls, removed for rotting in place in front of harsh tongues spitting bitter sweet lies in the faces of comrades, the men behind the lines, digging trenches and carrying arms. Your brother or your sister one of them, or the remains. Two aluminum plates etched then pulled from chains, no longer around severed necks as topless their bodies remain from the fifty caliber shell shot straight from the hell fire of a ten-ton machine built to destroy all that we've created or a forty mega-ton mushroom blast that incinerates a hundred miles upon contact. And they never saw it coming. Nor did we. Only the man behind the button and the four fourteen-digit codes chained to another man's arm. It's not his arm carried through those holes dug. His finger held silently, cold, limply over a depressed red switch. Who is to call that war? War for humanities sake? I think not. What happened to chivalry with white knights wielding broad silver swords? It's been replaced by black nights wielding thin crimson stained spikes. Hopeless romantics with their poetry died in the years before we realized the ozone was fried. The hole seemingly growing bigger like the whole of our race. Looking to the cosmos we begin to dwindle in space. Our spark losing its light as we use every last drop of our sulfurous energy to fuel our next high of amnesia so kind. No longer use the mind but let the drugs do the talking. For insanity is only sweet when society is forgotten. One must let go of all to be free but that is insanity and synonymous with death. Yet still strive to live free, to walk the edge without falling into the pit for despair brings only desperation and in desperation fingers clutch too close too tight. That is why she will leave you tonight. Free spirits cannot be contained. The tighter you squeeze, the further they run until, as again, you are all alone; crouched in back alleys beneath rotted wooden planks for a roof out of the drizzling rain from the bleak grey sky.

I can't remember the last time I took the time to appreciate the glory of the sun rising on our world. Took the time to actually feel the shadows disperse and warmth flood back into the landscape I oh too often look over as my path heads on. I'm happy to stop my life and its direction for a minute or ten or an hour or more to again see just how beautiful the sky can be as clouds drift my way waving hello with the firm morning cry of an early bird's song. So blue and crisp after purple haze that puts me in a daze of blinding beauty that graces our stratosphere. I find myself longing again to be as this tree that with wisdom sits and grows next to me. To see the sunrise on a hundred years or more. Greet me with your life. Make me strong by your light. Wrap me tight in heaven's delight. Oh sun, what a poet you make my heart wont to be for I could stare at you all day and miss not the moon. Why have I forgotten your touch? Why have I not partaken of your beauty more often? I lust for you sweet sun in devilish blue sky because you coax mine eye with beauty so rare and unique every time. Never once have I seen you rise the same nor set so sorrowfully from my whispering kisses as you fall to sleep at night. Oh how I have missed my sun so bright. Thank you for always holding me tight. For with you I could share anything. You will not judge, just offer me light. You will not falter nor fail nor destroy me for my lack of insight. But with warm fingertips you will keep my spirits up. You will warm my face, warm my heart and now as I sit and stare you start. Pulling over the horizon, your light basks me now. So bright, so blue, alive and new – again – You are born, and as always with it you bring a new day.

And then the slow waves come. Encompassing existence. Just a slow lull. We almost want to call them the doldrums. Just a kind of peace. Like the desert as it breaks for sunset, or that glorious sunrise where that golden orb takes siege on the skies. Taking up with its glorious forever extending arms the whole of the earth as its child. A baby in its mothers arms. And the ocean rolls to the tempo of that mother rocking her baby into a comforting state of euphoria. Just that peace that picks you up. It picks up the pieces. Makes what was once whole and then destroyed whole again with a new strength. A new balance of equilibrium to match the harmonious symphony of the universe playing with my life. And my life idly playing in this playground of existence. We call this life. And to live – be joyous. For this is the god's child-play. We are what our makers envision. We are that part of ourselves. That part that we perceive. Let us envision not only today, not only ourselves, not only life, but let's envision tomorrow. Let's make the future as brilliant and dynamic as those sun's rays diluting through tarred window panes. Let's not stop with the simple. Let us be glorious in the kingdom that we build together. Let there be no end to the rivers of happiness that course through our time. Let there be no end to the waves of our deep oceans of emotion as we feel and interact with a thousand faces that we have named our friends. And let them be not alone in any moment where their heart cannot carry them on its dove like wings. Let us hopeless romantics never die. Let us still fuel the fire for the "lost emotion." It's in you. You can feel it as do I. Take hold. Don't let that slip away. Don't let any of it fall from your swaying grasp because you hold the happiness of your own existence in your own subtle hands. As the clay that is is. Form it. Shape it into a better reality then what has been shown before your revolving eyes. Look, look, look at everything around it. Enjoy the dynamics. Enjoy the diversity. Taste the freedom.

Misty skies lurk between my eyes and those fertile mountain tops. A blinking red light the only movement in the night air. A gentle breeze too weak to lift hanging leaves cools my skin while candles burn before me and the pages of my mind. This pouring red ink mirrors my thoughts. The ink that has become my vent. My relief. A place where I can seemingly be free away from the chains of societies grasp. Where my wings can open and I can soar high above the worlds inside. A new perspective taking me away from the congestion and the smog. A new high.

I once looked into a mirror not realizing it was a mirror. I asked myself "who is that looking at me?" As I moved the man followed my movements and I realized that man was me. Objectively I didn't even recognize myself. It's funny how perspectives work. You can study something so long and know exactly what you are seeing but until you have the right perspective you can't truly see what you are seeing. How can you interpret what you are seeing for what it is unless you have the right state of mind? I saw a man for a moment that I didn't recognize but as soon as I attributed my attributes to his form I recognized myself. That's how I see all of life. You have to put the right attributes to what you are seeing before you can interpret and recognize what is before you.

How do you know a candle, until it is burning?
How do you know a tree until its leaves are turning?
How do you know a tear until your face is wet?
How do you know a smile until your face is set?
How do you know a cold until you sneeze?
How do you know a bird until you see a dove?
How do you know love?

Am I good, am I evil? Am I both, am I neither? Where does the dichotomy end? Where do I begin? What tales told on tongues no longer young, no longer bold. What stories spoke in verse, in song, or in deed. Heed the lessons if you dare, if you care, if the words a'flight float softly into yearning ears. How many years of stories spoke hasten to this my pen, my forsaken friend. The tales of deeds not to speak of by hands too coarse to care. A flip a swirl, a word with flare. As the eyes of the listeners stare upon the speaker daring themselves to glare as the horrors untold unfold and unfurl appearing to discerning eyes the deeds of a man's darker side. The hate the rage, the consuming lust. Dust and cobwebs brushed from volumes never told. Pages not marked only dogeared as fears and failures come to light with each turning from the spine. To listen and ask why dark pasts are brought to light. Dark nights trolled in old shoes nothing more than another stranger's plight. Open windows, locked doors. Blinds pulled tight to hide from the sight of a stranger's stare. Moving stories on screens or pictures in imagination a lit with candlelight. Hidden, hidden, one and all from sight. Amidst the blindness, feet on parole, hands softer in time help lift new souls. Talents and ambitions still ripe upon the vine. Fruiting and waning waiting to be plucked in time. Nourishing words drop like dew dancing from tongues gaily and sublime. Words that dance in rhythm. Words that find their rhyme. And ears that hear and yearn to grasp that which is of the essence, not of the past. And so a man unfolds. Naughty by nature as we all are wont to be. Caring and nurturing as we all soon shall be. Dichotomies of nature, the sinner and the saint. Truth has no bounds inside the stories that we paint. Touch the tales the storyteller speaks. Remember the rules and always what's at stake. The truth of a man in his stories told. The fate we all face in the mirrors of this place.

What a putrid stench the city doth exude into the clear night air, unnoticed by lovers doing what lovers do in the comfort of their homes between satin sheets next to dimly flickering candles that burn in the breeze of open windows. Foul and hot cigarette smoke fills and wafts from my lungs in grey puffs of insomnia. 'Tis another night in my mind in a foreign place visited but not yet seen. Written into this book of mixed thought and callous emotions. I once read about the thoughts of a woman's mind written into her "chronicles of masturbation" and fruitful thoughts filled my mind of how my ink must flow onto these pages. Pure thoughts she wrote tainted not by societies charms and drawn naught towards popular demand. The truth of her being poured from her soul in ink onto lined pages. Scribbles she wrote in incomplete thoughts as I wondered what she was thinking. Tonight is a night sequeling a day of learning. Where I learned of women, of men and of beast. What beasts that take harbor within the shells of ourselves, our bodies, our minds. Perchance it be only my mind that within dwelleth such beasts of no reason. Knoweth any man what driveth idle hands to play? Music made by those hands crasheth tremulous symbols into resonating sanity and strum high pitched chords on thin, taught metallic wires with a feverish pitch towards a chaotic forte crescendo. All is well without sleep as my mind stirs restlessly to and from within the cavity of my skull. Too many questions arise to answer within the nights of no sleep.

Sitting here looking at a five page tree remembering as it grew from leaf to leaf. Not a whisper among the branches now that you could say reside in solidarity. Fear and consternation choking out the memories of new emotions. What can be said to that tree? Its leaves alive and yearning but for the sun of another's day. Dead emotions, burnt to ashes stirred with seed and stick until with breath it breathes and fills its lungs thick. Yet, still alone, kin has no roots so near or deep. Rainfall trickles, drunk for sustenance, weeped as tears. Green, like the newborn it is, cheeks flushed with red as the rivulets disperse in time. Heat and passion and emotion as fire contained burning from the inside out seeking for a way to shout and be heard. Cues are missed, or lost, or once then always forgotten so that deaf awaiting ears with yearning, yearn in vain of the silence wrought by pain. Yet no disdain and no refrain. No chorus, nor verse, nothing rehearsed only a passion that cannot be contained and is long wont to be let out.

Of vice, of men and of women we play. Dance in solitude in solidarity like mice as men or of mice and men. But not thrice blind. Must we remind ourselves of what it is we seek? Answers only questions hidden so deep. To touch or taste is to know one's self and never know anything else. What portraits that are painted 'cross the blue skies, dark at night, city-scape, blinding star light. Like children bold and without fright chewing the fat, gnawing the bone. Marrow once lost and now not found but sought with fervor without grace. Stumble, trickle, fall; Least these things are no crimes that we can thrust behind walls. Rooftops and greenhouses, ladies and men on display. But no foreplay. No kiss, no touch, no caress. No dismissing of another's dress. No hand holding, no locked eyes. No dreams igniting. No fireworks, no new skies. No new heights, only new limits. Another lost chance. Regret that won't diminish. What must be found is locked in Paradox. A land well known to the bumbling ox. Virtuous perhaps – within his own mind. Destroyer of dreams only some of the time. Hardly foolhardy for not having the most common of sense, yet still hands lay idle to drum, twirl or debate. Eyes closed, mind yearning. Yet another hour has grown late. Another through the third until it showers outside revealing no tears, reveling in sunshine. No consumption in that moment by all old years. Callous without malice. Coarse yet so fine. Truth through pain as there's pain through the truth. Perhaps we'll never know what trees may dare if we never pick up the....

Pillar upon pillar stacked high in ascending order towards a blue grey sky. Lit stars golden harboring atop the pillars of gold blackened in time and use. Rusty hands scaling the bricken walls to the castle's turrets. Archers long since arrows shot passed away, bodies lying empty as skeletons charcoal grey or pasty white. Moonlight only forgiving to the eye for such moments not seen. Slept under gently on cracked cobblestone or in fields of dewy pastures grazed nimbly by lively livestock drinking of life as each new day becomes the same without change. Seemingly as it should be yet not exactly making the coherence hence desired. Not all things of sense make, for making cents takes hard word. Maybe harsh mouths millionaires make or just tasting of lies tender meat gnawed on then spit out in good taste, but no good faith. For what faith in lies can one bestow? Is not the lie truth's worst foe. But to say truth is to say not which one knows but to know for knowing's sake. The sake to not be fake when the temptation arises for smiles have a personality much of their own devices. One which is pure the other is none. How many lies are too many when one is never enough? One, two, or three? Just olives in a martini. Any more is a can of worms not to be opened for the stench of living dirt from dead corpses remains dried and dusted causeth such pain to nasal passages before and under eyes not so kind, lost in faith, thus blinded and never sated for one lie is never enough.

Searching for an awakening. Always longing for true knowledge of the self. Not only in me but everyone as well. Blank pages marked by a crimson pen are the prisms of the mind feeding thoughts into a photographic kaleidoscope. Repressed memories become daydreams in the insomnia filled nights of weeks passing by into years of long lost millenniums. Tomorrow seems gone before the waking of today. Before the wake of my life. The end of a multi-forked road. Frost's roads less traveled by, trampled by the feet who run in contemplative circles. Indecisiveness becomes the decision for this and afore moments. Space is the dwindling holes of consciousness. Emotions drowning out seclusion with their frustrating dances. The sparring agony and pleasure oil the hands tightly squeezing hard metallic rails of sanity's vertigo. I sit alone at night on the same rooftop. What stories the night holds for me.

Explorations. Where we travel through our mind as we envision and perceive the world around us. Slowly to the right steadily held. Green with life, green with envy. Cold but bright. Rustling gently together back and forth from right to left. Turned ever up thirsty, hungry, yearning. Tall, slender, alive. Strongly standing firm set in place on the ground reaching higher for the sky. To reach that golden orb. How much alike mortal man is to the mortal tree. To feel yourself planted in this world from seeds. To feel nature's calling forces. Inspiration, divination. Everything grows towards opposite poles. Towards the sky, towards the center of the earth. Trying to fill the spaces in between with it's existence. Surviving so that you too can shed your seed and your energy can live on long after your roots have dried up and leaves withered. What is a memory? Where is it held? How is it seen? Where do they come from, how are they born into our minds? Why do they affect us shaping our realities? No matter how I live my life my memories will always be the same leading me to the same end. it's no longer the means to an end but an end of means. Interpolation of meaning in subjective narcissism. Who we are and why we are that way is however we interpret it to be. In essence who you are is you in your eyes through the eyes of everyone else. There is no meaning. There is no understanding. My life is about adding, to the memories that which they are lacking. To add intemperance throughout. To fill my cup of Circe. To become the Sardanapalus of man, of myself. To solace the vexation in my mind. To remember how I want it to be as opposed to how it was.

Hope is
that substance which keeps your idle mind awake in anticipation at
night.

Hope is
why you light a candle to see in the dark with your last match.
It's what grabs your chin pulling roughly up casting your eyes to the
stars when you are too tired to sleep on that asphalt rooftop.
It's the forgotten pain in your legs as your eyes pull you closer to your
home.

It's the quarter you drop in the payphone to call home when
no one is there and you know it.

Calm before the storm
Silence speaks, we can't hear it
Still outside the void
Deaf and dumb we don't know
Lost within the eye
Playing games we can't name them
Burn inside the storm
Where we go we just don't know

Calm before the storm
The tides change we can't see it
Still outside the void
Blind and lost we don't grow
Lost within the eye
Blinking fast we can't frame them
Burn inside the storm
Unseeing where do we go?

Calm before the storm
Rhythm's lost we can't feel it
Still outside the void
Broke and numb, we won't show
Lost within the eye
Pins and needles we can't tame them
Burn inside the storm
Apathy will break us down

What songs you sing to me in thought, in word in deed. Men forget often what women always remember, but our tables have turned proven by a heart shaped ring lonely on the dresser top. Placed on your finger by my own hand. Taken off in my absence as you travel 'cross the land. What you do when you are gone I have no clue but misplaced jewelry replaced with sweet perfume troubles this forgetful man. You say I read to deep and that is why I weep. Nay, I say, I cry when I care and it is with my eyes I see and care too much about the forgotten things replaced with lipstick and blush. How pretty you may be for your friend long lost and how sweet smelling you must seem to that forgotten nose under the eyes that gleam. A jealous man I may seem. Let the truth be known for in honor I cannot sleep worrying with a troubled heartbeat at why oh why the heart shaped ring you do not wear to proclaim your love for me.

Look at that sexy girl lounging before your eyes. Wonder then realize the meaning of tough love. Not sweet romanticism but the passion of pounding flesh. The abandonment of depth where the flesh becomes the last vessel from soul to mind. Where senses excel with euphoric chemicals that chart paths through an already ransacked cardiovascular system. A ransacked mind that thinks no more about thinking and more about aesthetic pleasure because that is the designer drug coursing through your shot system. Insomnia no longer a disease – just a drug to keep your eyes ever parted so that not one minute of life is lost in hindsight. An observer of the world can stand high and free on his pedestal of grandeur. He can see the tops of the mountains and the peaks and valleys of life. But what does he really see? These people before him. Who are they? Could he touch their soul if he really tried or is that the lost part of our humanity? The part we have forgotten in ancestors once alive now dusty corpses that rattle in the base of our spine like those church bells ringing before the hymns of our new time are sung by the voices of so many who are just as lost as the rest of us. And do they sing to themselves, for themselves or are their hearts more pure? Do they sing praise to some "giver of life" whose face remains to be shown for only by true faith are we granted passage to what we know not. Then the question comes – what do we really know? Do you know yourself? Do you know your mind or do you just know the tastes tantalized on your tongue. Then we come to realize that knowing is not the problem, but living is. We live to learn, to work, and to strive on to an end that is inevitable trying to fight every second of last call away so that the night doesn't end. So that we may continue and experience just once more a warm embrace held or an endearing trance like stare between our lovers and ourselves. And we fight so hard for those things every moment of our life with more failure than success. But oh the sweet taste in the adventure of it all. The sweet smell in capture and the pleasure evoked forever from resilience and growth in our own forsaken prosperity.

I walked by haphazardly seeing your form there in my bed. My pillow warm in your rest. As I came back by I saw the emptiness of my room and the pillow twisted through empty blankets on my bare bed. No warm embraces 'neath satin sheets of gold. No castle, no clouds, no picket fence. There are no more lies bestowed upon two dilating eyes in silvery mirrors projected home to myself. No more mirrors to see what is transparently grey. No more justifying the means by the end when the means are the end. All of creation, all that is created, is born from a death. The end of something great always becomes the beginning of something better and so the wheel of life turns as the wheel of fortune. The stakes are raised. The risk is great. Chances and lifelines are thrown out for haste. Hasten to what is the question. Merely a panter of mind's eye lies awake even at noon or ten or nine or by twos or threes, being the key, by six and nine so we begin to define divine. Mathematicians and philosophers, psychologists and linguistics, religion and death are all the same as insanity or what we once thought was normal is no longer in question of stability or growth. Yet a tree grows with life as do words in black ink on white pages torn, not shredded, from wear of use not years of dusty cobwebs hiding the shame, the guilt we fear in absence of pain. Truth be posed or grimly decided, reality becomes one of our vices. To look back, to remember, to forget divine. For this is the line we walk on the edge of tomorrow as today carries on its shoulders the burden of our paths. Leave strewn or broad, riverside or picturesque none is concerned for a feather that falls up in the wind may never touch the ground where tears were shed. Fresh spring water no red hue but blue and clear and strong like summer wind of winter's song. Cold as ice as mountain tops of frozen white. Rainbow to rainbow no prisms in between we are free men learning to live to love. No bondage thus remains on Icarus's wings. Remember only the wax of that candle melts only as long as the wick that burns. Energy to energy reaction to action but only one action took place.

Life.

Have you ever been so intrigued as when you ponder the shape of your new lovers artistic slender fingers? And when is it – that moment when you become lovers? Is it that first embrace or stolen kiss from wet hot lips or the first penetration of body into body. Yet maybe aesthetics plays a non-vital part. Maybe it's that enchanting glance that forces your hand – makes you say hello when truly you are still afraid of reproach. Maybe it's just wistful dreams set afire from that tongue taunting you to listen to its tales. Listen to its heartbeat course through the marrow in your ear echoing its discord throughout your mind which can merely search for freedom of societies calamity. Maybe you don't know and all you do is search and make excuses so that this odd world seems more reasonable and more understandable even amidst your tremulous confusion.

Let me enjoy the comfort of your sweet embrace. Gingerly wrap your soft arms around the hardness of my flesh. Let me taste your sex and every inch of your curvature as you comfort my ears with low moans and heavy wanton breathing. I have always enjoyed the taste of your breath hungrily fed to me between the conflict of our lips dueling out an abandon-less search for one another's soft wet texture. Don't hold back a thing as you wrap the fleshy part of your thighs around me. Let me tickle gently the button minutes before caressed by my prying fingers as they parted the outer folds of your lavish and moist garden. I can taste the dew of your essence on my tongue as it rubs roughly against your inner folds. I enjoy with fervor every drop of your essence lingering in the recesses of my mouth as you let me take you. As you let me enter you and defile your body in the most pleasurable positions that our united flesh can endure.

With a look just right and eyes so keen. I wonder at the wonders you have seen. What is it like to know you in the flesh? Are you the best? Cherished could you be? Could you be free? Or is alone your home, solitude your friend, silence your mother, holding you tight in slumber. What does your naked skin look like in sunlight? If bare would you bare all or would you cross your legs in fear and despair. The morality of the moment lost in hindsight of a night for pleasure. Pleasure sought or evoked, on your body my body strokes. What do these hands tell you as your flesh they endear and caress. Fingers touch lightly after nails rake skin to remember again the life before them as they feel a pumping yearning vessel longing to be freed in touch. Be free to sensuality. Be free to passion because compassion takes too long. It's a song we sing into the wee hours of midnight gone. What a symphony of moving flesh our bodies make when there is no haste. A slowly drawn chord on a violin's strings of love. But no love can be found so fast and furious – only pleasure. And again we reminisce of the diversity that exists between us that keeps us apart. That keeps me from knowing you in the flesh. Such rifts that exist merely for style hidden behind kind (but not true) smiles. The tasks of the day come too easily with practice and repetition. What we really want to say and what we really mean is forgotten in the habits of social games. You speak of sex so loud but that's not what I'm hearing. I'm hearing that sex is no option that your flesh is closed to a vagabond's touch. Your flesh could receive a traveler's embrace but not open they'd never see your true face. Not many travelers, though, enjoy your succulence because you believe your standards are higher until the time comes when the need overwhelms you and you submit to your natural desires. The natural calling forces that are farther embedded into you then your morals only once conceive and believed. Pull your shirt up again and hide from my eyes the beauty of your pale skin. Hide from me all you want. Show me not the caress of your eyes. Show me not what you hold in the palm of your hand, my heart. Show me not your life but make small talk to appease my ears of hearing your sweet voice that I long to hear moaned in my ears. Whisper to me as I sit inside of you hard and long and full. Beg for me to give you pleasure, want my touch more then anything else for that excites me most. Beg to be released in orgasm and beg for my essence. Ask me to come and by two beats of my heart I will. Let me take you to form different shapes with our united flesh. Let our bodies feel each others every part. Look in my eyes, touch my soul, feel me grow and grow. Hold me tight, all through the night, never let go, never give up. Love my every part it's all I could ask, it's all I shall know, it's all I want. But today is not that day nor tomorrow, that is true sorrow. But in time I will find you. In time you will find me and then we shall be free. I long to be free. Find me fast I beg and plead for how much longer can I last without being cherished by you.

Thine eyes sparkle like soft candlelight.
The flip of thy hair whispers pleasure through the night.
Thy gentle touch sends shivers down my spine.
For thee my lady are the love of mine.
If thoust knew the songs sang to me from thy fingers tips,
traversed across our souls between embracing lips.
Then solemn chords of angels ring.
Upon our hearts whilst of love they sing.
It is the harmony of orchestra reflected in thy voice to my yearning ears.
That leaves the chorus of our love for the remainder of our years.
The sea's color caught in thine fine eyes so pale,
pulls my soul from my heart till all my love doth wail for thee.
Dost thou know what thou hast done to me?
As I fall to the ground upon my knee.
Kneeling before my angel of lore,
I hand thee the key to my heart's door.
Across the threshold thy whispering feet doth lay.
To my awaiting embrace where I hold thee steady.
In love our bodies do all but join.
In making love we become but one.
Thy heartbeat I feel against my bosom
as thine body shakes with a soulful orgasm.
Thou hast become the meaning of my life
so it matters not if it be day or night
for thee I fight!
And with my life, I would pay.
To hold thee again upon this day.
To feel the freedom in thy kiss.
The sweet ambrosia of which is softer then bliss.

How does one know love when it is gone? Silently sitting in repose – cheek inches away from open lips, parted in breath so humble. Emotions drowned out so long with enumerating thoughts until memories themselves – tarred and feathered – become black and white reruns without technicolor. But yet we see and must wonder if the color of love is blue or green or red. Was it real, alive or merely dead. Black roses or red or pink in life. Lost and withered now watered back to bloom. Little buds from little seeds nourished in soft earth. Two proverbial hands clasping textured dewy petals caressing and appeasing. Was beauty therein seen or realized or merely demoralized. Touched and tasted. The pistol and the pollen dropped between soft pink petals parted 'neath the rays of a harvest sun. Thorns so thick and razor sharp only the gentlest of holding hands – in rhythm torn apart – beseech such lips worn ragged and weak. Dry and thirsty searching for another taste of heaven, of bliss, of your kiss. Torn at the cracks, creased at the seams, broken and blistered without the nectar of their queen-bee. Such honeycomb passed through on a pegasus' wings in flight, in rapture, in love's sweet fright. The long well thorned stem penetrates calloused skin on rugged fingers worn procuring blood, and loss and absence of hate and scorn. Yet in mist of starry nights, much sleep begot in dewy fields of nature's wild. In growth tomorrow another child is born. With petals soft and so divine two came together to form one mind. In its birth there was you and me, but now miles from the sea we have grown into us.

If I could write one page of prose for every teardrop shed in my life,
what a poet I would be.
Thousands of stories could be told without ever letting
understanding reach another soul.
If I could shed one tear for every night slept alone,
volumes I could add to that work of grace
without ever seeing another's face.
If I could dream one good dream for every day I spent in love,
I'd never have a nightmare cross the threshold of my sleep
for the rest of my life.
If one candle burned for one minute for every hour of pain
I felt in my heart,
there would be enough light to write my life's story on
a hundred different nights.
If I could smile just once for every moment of happiness then
I would finally smile for a day.
But if I could remember just one thing,
I would have to remember your smile.
One moment of happiness
seen in your eyes
is worth
a thousand stories of my pain.

What is it about   a   butterfly that turns
       your mind in circles   making you think of
           so many things. You   can feel sunshine on
          your face when you see a butterfly's wings.
             Yet somewhere in your heart you long
                  to crawl from your own cocoon
                        to fly. Yet you fear your
                    wings would be clipped. You
                  fear you won't blend in anymore
         with that safe leaf you nibble on for survival.
         But how beautiful it would be to taste freedom as
      it rushed under your wings lifting you lightly into air.
   Not as a bird with   a   cage as a home. But your

feet gently resting on soft petals that soak you from their pistol. Cold
dew drops on soft green grass cleansing you of your sins. Every day a
new day begins with a sunrise in the heavens and a harvest of the land.

Sitting here long past twilight. Red and large strawberries unfolding in my mouth, the sweet and bitter juices dancing on my tongue remind me of our night together. Our mouths exploring one another for the first time only to move on to other parts. Fervent mouths, reverent in their simple embraces. Lavished moistly against each other time and time again. Sometimes with the quick brush of tongue. Sometimes a linguistic dance. Hands unable to lay idle caress and embrace or pull closer to unite a burning beneath the flesh. Skin upon skin, a membranes embrace, a dance with the devil, a tongue to taste. Even after the long day with no respite your taste and touch lingers upon me and I hope to never wash it away. It keeps fresh in my mind that long luxurious line that was from your breast to your hips down your legs to your toes' tips. The line of a body drawn and shaped, contoured against mine in a long embrace. No better could I have imagined in my mind. The scent of you lingers trapped in my pillows and sheets. Already I loathe laundry day when I must wash the last essence of you that in my apartment remains – away. I must invite you back to replenish my supply of all that I see in you that makes me smile. Your kind eyes open, deep and bright. Your hair soft and styled to my finger's delight. Your lips striated, cupped between mine. Kissed again and again as to disperse time. The hands that I remember, fingers aloof. Clasping me sensually proving one truth. Body-lines and curves pressed tightly to mine, I could never get enough. There is no such thing as time enough. Smile when you read this. Remember my taste. Don't forget my hands nor their rough embrace. Remember my eyes that you looked into so much, remember their look, remember their touch. Remember my lips and all that they did, their best and their worst and the tongue that they hid. Remember me as much as you can. Remember this sensual complicated man. But of all things I want for you to remember most – is the way in which we kissed. Of that we can always boast.

The light within the dark. The spark within the life. Billiards and beer. Dreams and fears. Just one unforgettable night. The butterfly touches, nothing more then glancing blows, you know not the way the light in your eye glows. A voice telling stories trying to whisper amidst the din. Finding too late one more friend. Again we begin as we begin to end. The start too late as we approach the last bend. If ever I could ask time to stand still. This moment or that a hug against the chill. The night air so brisk, my pace too fast, always doomed to risk making a regrettable past. One foot in, one foot out, decisions to make, we rise to our fate. The promise of another night and sight for sore eyes. The beauty in a face opined on from afar. The taste so keen on tongues never born. The anticipation of things that shall not form. A purse, a pout, a smile and a tremble. Hesitation it seems will make me humble. How do I get so near while still so far apart. When may I kiss your lips to feel the beating of your heart. When will you blush and put aside your restraint? When will you submit without complaint? A fingertip's stroke from your temple to your chin. The brush of my thumb across your lips and within. Open your mouth; take in some air. Prepare yourself for what I dare. My humble existence hinging upon my need. To taste the taste of your lips, to swallow your mouth's mead. The honey, the essence, the nectar of the gods. Nothing more than our tongues at odds. A push, and a pull, a soft stroke with the tips, daring ourselves to never part lips. Three seconds in time become infinite. As I awake from my dream to find my lip but bit. The drop of blood a reminder of what could not be. A kiss, just a kiss, to set me free.

You can listen to the truth or you may believe the lies. When the freedom of choice possesses you, take a path and decide. Be it the high road or the forlorn. Listen to the storytellers and follow along. Don't forget the sides of the path that, narrow and dark, encroach tighter and tighter until only a thin thread remains. Balance precariously but dare not run. No longer you will have to hold something tight as your arms flail at the sides trying to keep a drunken balance so frail. A simple wind blown on a kiss from gentle lips pursed mockingly tight. Pressed to my forehead underneath straight brown locks draped to halo my existence with an angel's face. Fallen you have become teetering no longer on the lies faded in time until dispersed like cobwebs under brush fire. There is a fire that burns with me only hands scorched as I clutch tight that which no one shall cherish for I am not a storyteller. My words are not so kind in flight to ears open hungry for lies. My words are black arrows of truth piercing through the games destroying the masks revealing all faces that have hid in shame the nature of themselves from all the worlds races because they too know that only the masks survive in this world of no regard. Whom hath regarded the reality of this moment or any other. Time may erase pain but it also paints the masks in darker colors. Yellow becomes orange then red and green to blue and violet until blackened dead a hundred years in the making. Wrinkles wasted on fake smile. Crows feet telling the tales of false laughter at jokes not humorous only another good story to help us forget ourselves. Once, twice, a hundred times removed. So far from truth, ourselves we become as day in and out we are asked to lie so we may succeed. When all lie, then all die. For truth knows only life and eternity. Lies know only death. The end of creation is a thousand lies unwilling to repent and speak true that which makes "I" me. I dare not wrinkle the coarseness of my face from time and lies and all this shit. I want to be me and free and true for you.

Why?

Because I love, I care, I am me.

A spider, in stillness, suspended in time. Legs akimbo, waiting to dance. My greatest foe, together locked in trance. Him the hunter, now my muse. A bite so vicious as want to leave a bruise. A sting, just a peck, from a razor like beak. Two claws, one bite, the pain may last a week. Eyes not needed, it feels the slightest stirring. Its web not of deceit but a trap all the same. The blood sucker waiting. Head towards the floor amidst invisible thread, silent and still. No fear, no dread. A fly on a path for sustenance's embrace. The dance macabre only moments away. Ushered away from cold milk to another silken embrace. Quick legs down the lines to a treasure trove of flesh to wrap and to hold as one that loves you best. Back to its young. Back to its nest. Let the feast begin. My foe the spider consumes yet another's flesh.

I watch and I learn, I realize my place.

Not in front nor behind, to the left nor the right, but together alone.

One love, one life, one night.

All of his life he has learned to weave a web. He has learned how and where to hunt. All day his web grew and grew in the most perfect place. With bold determination he cast his net as far as he dared hoping to have the best spot and the biggest feast. The dance of life, him taking others, creating balance by foregoing abundance. The spider eats the flies that are too many. So why when I see his legs suspended in air do I shirk away? Why do I flinch? Why must his life be snuffed out? Why must he die? The dance of life. Me taking his life creating balance by foregoing abundance. Too many spiders. Yet I envy his patience as he sits so still. Hour after hour waiting for his meal. What will he think when it all comes to an end?

Thank you for inspiration, for life, for a friend.

All good things must come to an end.

Even the life of a spider.

His present long, she blowing lightly
Listen as her chill dropped for dark wind
Are fathered snow like march and as a winter fling?
What can ask about early waves?
Throw balm - Let a week out
Have blesser feeling there - even I am off
Was odd day Leave it from ever - yet over as read

Why go?
                    Fall
          Shadow -
                    see empty dreams
          You breath sky -
                    use luscious hours
                    where all this
                    deep blue morning moon
                    wanders to the cold earth.
          Through my sleep,
                         Love
                    will need a summer rain -
          Hurry
                    Lie openly -
                    curve -
                    dance -
                    Surrender,
                    Murmur,
                    Remember
                    You are the year after
                    Begin a song with time -
          How these hear a stormy moment turn
                    Like one child
                         (friend)
                    Gentle – less sunny
              .   spring star,
                         warm him,
                         tell him not,
                    Mother shall come -
                         be green here
                         and
                         gold vanishes.

79

Just as suddenly she turned the corner and disappeared behind the tall building. Quickly, with not a doubt in my mind, I strode in the direction that she lead. One hand casually swinging at my side with my other comfortably in my pocket. The cars slowed as I lazily crossed the street in a determined yet uncaring pace. The soft soles of my shoes, not making a sound on the pavement, sought their path in the wake of – "her". My clothes rustling softly from the movement of my body, the only whispering sound in my ears. I longed to look once again at the beauty that fate had shown my rugged eyes. As I rounded the same corner at which she turned, I saw her. Standing there looking in my direction. Almost as if she was waiting for my arrival. A smile creased my face ever so slightly and my steady eyes bored deep into hers. Into her soul. She blinked rapidly before a faint smile found its way to her lips. I walked straight towards her my eyes unwavering and my gate steady and strong. I stopped in front of her no more then a foot away. The strong sweet scent of her perfume enveloped my senses and overwhelmed the putrid stench of the polluted city. I inhaled her scent deeply for a moment, enveloping my senses with her essence. She looked at me expectantly waiting for me to speak for she herself was wordless beneath my gaze. I let the power of silence rule for a moment longer allowing her to become even more mystified by my presence. Then she opened her mouth to speak and I raised a finger to her agape lips to stop the breath in her chest before it could make song. When the tip of my coarse finger brushed her soft lips a sigh escaped her mouth instead of words. I leaned closer to her and I knew she yearned for my kiss. Instead my lips brushed her ear and I whispered ever so slightly,

"I want you".

Then her mouth opened again and I turned away and strode off into the midst of the crowded city never to see her beauty again.

He trips a thousand dreams. A symphony of visions to worship. A whisper, sad, black, and elaborate. Bear my eternity of madness! The moment drives moonless like her tongue panting white visions. Misted and singing I am a shadow. Flooded with the ugly storm. Moaning bitter love and screaming drunken sordid language. Manipulated petal is death to rose. Incubate beauty but live as the wind.

If there was a garden of Eden and Adam and Eve populated the world with their seed, then artists were spawned from Eve. They are the sons and daughters of she who seeked enlightenment. The sons and daughters of Adam are societies children. Raised as sheep to look in awe at the splendor of life's passageways, unveiled through thick rose colored glasses the artists have removed for perfect perception. Carnality is truth and justice. Morality the foe of freedom. What religion has tried to accomplish becomes a cage while the spirit spits out for freedom. Freedom of self from binding clauses of right and wrong. The subconscious feeds our mind's eye with freedom's truth. Sins are reality while hymns lock you in. No man is without sin yet not all men are free. What do artists do but taste freedom as a sweet chardonnay or a Dom Perignon while the grapes of wrath drown Adam's children in an airy merlot. A vinaigrette no sweeter then bitter entrapment. The voyeur is nothing more than an exhibitionist who fears freedom. Anyone can look and watch. Everyone does. But who unveils for the eager crowds other then the free spirited artist whose shame lies not in the flesh nor the mind, but in an ancestry where its next of kin has waged wars for the freedom they could have had if only they too removed the spectacles to see the spectacles before them. Time erases pain, not bondage nor chains. Each link tightening its grip as people crawl to the back of their cages away from the unmorality they see in the freedom they so desire.

Why must the fruit of the young be so sour? Why such bitter tastes acquired from those most desired? Lips not true looking chakras like blue, so limp and cold from coercion. What you say? Your way? All day, show me the way, I'll feel free to pay. No cash left, but a torn body I'll waste for haste in life to death through deeds only once conceived as fun, and you say you're the only one. But too many out there to be all alone just a horoscope's dot on the sky. No more freedom in space 'cause you lost your grace to the ways of the world so blind. You my friend have the eyes of a hawk, but not true sight. You see well and you see far but blinded by your misled insights you take in no fright and reminisce of wrongs at will. Will you ever truly be free? Could you ever want a man like me? Real as can be, trying hard not to flee from your enchanting glance. Even when I know now is not my chance 'cause even my cage squeaks at night as I nibble alone the few breadcrumbs I have left to piss away. My friend, all days are new days, but no day compares in any way to the shape of tomorrow and yesterday. 'Cause where we come from and where we are going are just memories with no more glory. For each moment spent not in today is wasted away in our stories to reminisce on as we miss our song to the afterlife and preamble of today.

It is the unintentional misdemeanor we are all guilty of. It's the irrational behavior of logical concentration enveloping our minds. It's the one, two, three auto-man autopilot of flight through life. It's the dull-drums of stagnation through regression of face value of worth. It's of this and it's of that, but where are we really at? It's an emotional upheaval. It's the lost emotion. It's no motion. E-Motion. Motion through Ego. A subjective cause and effect roller coaster of force growing sparse. Thin and cracked it begins to fade in time until we lose our minds. 'Til we lose our masks and our games, we no longer remember our names or those of our neighbors so kind. Hiding from the blinding beauty of truth hidden and underlaid in everything, everyday, every way, in all minds. Freedom has no bounds and knows not space. Freedom is grace through life and ease of love felt shaking every man woman or child until they become wild again. Not living in the sin of tomorrow's yesterday, but anyway. Who are we? Who are you? Who is me? Just a man with a plan in the palm of his hand. Learning and living and loving and learning to live to love. Not above or below any man of this world. I'm just like you. I have no clue. No understanding of this world so vast as I watch it pass. Reposed on the proverbial ass of my mind, I sit and wonder why. The only answer is life and of life is beauty so keen sometimes mean playing with me. I traverse the path, I learn of my mind. Only in my knowledge do I but sin again. My friend, to know is to sin. It is the only sin of our times. The only crimes we commit in deeds of the mind. Lackluster dreams forgotten lore in my mind I open many doors. I look beyond; I try to strive on. I reach, I grasp, I learn, and I get burned. The wrath of truth is fierce and tough like a scar beneath the flesh burning its best. The scars of the flesh may last but a day but the scars of mind are lost in time. Forever they travel through space in any form until I forget that I know and become free. You see what it means to me, is to love for the sake of loving, for the sake of peace and tranquility so rare. Never fear. For we are in the times of the yesteryear. Where the future is born, today we fight! And in the night, we hold dear. And in the morning we shed no tears for every day is the beginning of a new day, new way. A way of life minus strife. A way of mind minus blind. To see, to love, to grow, to live to be free. So..

If I could write a song just what would I sing? How would the chorus go if I didn't know a thing? What would I say if a million words came to me? How would the story go and how would you be? Would you sit there and listen? Would you smile and reminisce? Would you laugh and joke and make fun of all of this? Would you taunt and tease and make fun of me or would you open your heart and learn to live free? Taking a flight into the mind we begin to transcend time. Leaving the past where it ought to be, behind of you and behind of me. We unlock the chains and begin to dance for this is life and this is our chance. With one beat flowing to the next rhythm hard our feet move so fast we have to discard the masks, the lies, the games we play, for this my friend is the beginning of a new day new way. New day, new way. No way to live locked away behind closed doors and false charades. Walk the parade, fall in line, but march to the beat of your own time. Not like a herd of sheep merely grazing but live your life with your mind a'blazing. Turn up the fire, turn up the heat, just clap your hands to the beat. Feel my rhythm, feel my flow, feel the world just so you know, where you stand and where you sit, what it is you're going to get. What it is your heart desires. Make sure you don't throw it on the pyre and make the smoke grow higher and higher. Smoke and mirrors masked adorned. We no longer know why we were born. The answer my friend is in this song. To live, to love, to get along. To learn to try, to fail and succeed 'cause that's the way it's going to be. Without love where would we be? I know I would not be me. Could not live free without love's wings, could not see all things shown to me. Just blind alone and desperate too, I honestly wouldn't know what to do. I'd sit here and cry and begin to die and ask myself why, oh why? Why ME? Why's it got to be like this? But like THIS, this is how it's got to be, when you open your heart and learn to live free.

He sits on those same brick steps tonight as he has so many nights before. The dim light feeding his eyes enough light to see the pages of the book before him that he occasionally reads and often writes in. The dim glow of his cigarette sparking between his slender fingers. His other hand grasping a pen with no cap. The ink oozes slowly from its tip as he presses it against yet another blank page. The smoke curls from his lips slowly after another puff. A Styrofoam cup sits by his side which he picks up every few minutes to sip the fluid from the clear plastic straw. His cigarette pack also lies by his side with a lighter resting on top waiting to feed his lungs with the nicotine his body craves. His knees pulled closely to his chin hold up that spiral book he writes in merely inches from his face. Long shadows cast about him in an orange hued light that hangs high upon the red bricked wall. All the thoughts churning in his mind as page after page he writes. His hands cup around the cigarette dangling from his lips and the lighter he sparks as he lights another cigarette. No one sees him there though he feels many eyes upon him. Narcissism the food for the egoist with an altruistic nature. His eyes look up and about him in thought as his pen pauses. And again as many nights before, he glances down again at the pages of his book before slowly folding it cover to cover sealing in the thoughts of another day.

So slow, so tranquil sitting in the grass with no breeze I stare at the glass of water serene before me. Little multicolored stars of synthetic light reflect up to me on this warm spring night. The air tainted lightly with a river's scent mixing with the taste of fresh green grass, not cut yet, but dewy and simple and alive under my ass. Not naked for in a public park my body sits in repose as my mind forgets to stop and pose only allowing a kaleidoscope of dreams to be thus displayed. For to be played. Which bring a word to mind – fortitude – or strength of being. Resilience to other forces that maybe I, nor no one, controls nor knows. And as the ducks fly to swim and splash and play as they have done all day I look up to watch their splendor. To better remember what life is about to me. Are they callous in their ways or just ruffled and mislead by breadcrumbs? Happy, they know not the word but displeased are they, nay. One swims towards my shore as if wanting to strike up a conversation but merely bantering me with the chorus of a duck's song. What would I hear if I could understand its cry? What stories would it tell me of its life. Would it tell me how it was raised of how many days it fought for shelter from the cold? Of how many storytellers it met with words of gold who dropped the snacks for it to enjoy because the men and women saw them as toys? What about the children that it ran from in fear because although they wanted to pet the little beasts how gentle could they really be? Their soft innocent laughter giggling from their bosom like adults too often mimic reminiscing about what can never be again. Would I hear the stories of how wings were caught in pain from a floating twig knocked out of a tree in the pouring rain that stuck close to their bosom 'til pulled away by a mother so kind she was always there. Would I hear about the webbed feet constantly in motion or how many fish were caught and what size and breed? Then again maybe I'd just hear quack-quack as they leave. If they were to fly back and land in my glassy landscape portrayed before my eyes and ears underneath a weeping tree that looks at its own multifaceted beauty in the reflection of a body of water trying to be a sea. But no buoyant salt to keep afloat lazy bodies not wanting to wash to shore. But silence is not heard in this night where my fingers touch the texture of small green blades sticky with the world's perspiration. The tree still sits, and sits still next to me looking over me as one of its own. For maybe I am its kindred and maybe one day my life will feed its roots to grow a sapling not unlike itself.

    A family of ducks in the night duck their heads under water to feast on more delights. They enjoy the hunt, they enjoy the catch it is all they have ever known. Maybe I am not so different as when I pick up the phone. Ducking for the hunt, hoping for the catch, relishing in the game of life. Sometimes I pause the screen of life to remember why I play. Sometimes I forget and keep on playing anyways. But as I remember and look up at the dark hued night sky to catch a glimpse of soft white clouds on my minds eye at peace I feel once again. For I am alive and part of all of this.

Sometimes you have to stand alone before a glorious panoramic picture to understand life without you. We all want to think that somehow our existence (or lack there of) will make a difference, a ripple, somewhere in this chaotic world that breathes, eats, and sleeps life. Sometimes when the light is around you just right and the darkness out there is hued with night you stop yourself from breathing because you don't want to disturb the perfection captured in this one moment just before the imperfect chaotic world rears its head and devours you in tomorrow's games. Tonight I have lost. I have lost myself in the games, in the drugs, in my words. I have lost the beating of my heart for it is not held tenderly by the grasp of someone for whom which I care. Yet I stare bleakly out into this night holding tight that which remains of me. My pen and my eyes and these hands that write. What may become of me will yet be seen. But 'tis too glorious a night to take in such fright and fear tomorrow's kiss. Because in each moment you make your own bliss. But who knows of this? Not you, nor him, nor her, nor I. I only see what is given to me and what I take. And what I take be not much for I have grown humble of aesthetic pleasures and journey more into my own mind. And if these are my adventures. Thus chronicled, thus laid. Then here they may lay to rest until the day they are swept away into tomorrow's tomorrow. Until there is no sorrow. Until all can be one. 'Til all can be free.

Anarchy: The lack of structure. A no-holds-barred world were anything goes and everything is left to chance.

Morality is the foe of freedom. Morality is not the base of structure, nor does structure create the foundation of morality. What a cultural society perceives as morals is dictated by what? Where the morals are created from is the greater question.

When morals are questioned and then tossed aside to fight, kill, and destroy for those "morals", is that morally correct? Or have we all blinded ourselves to our own faults with the false hope that we are right and everyone who does not agree is wrong because ancient texts say "our" morals are the only correct ones. Religion is in every culture of the world because no human's mind can comprehend our own existence. Thus our explanation(s) take the form of a higher power or god(s) whose hands have created and guide the path of our lives. Our every action thus dictated by the "morals" of our cultural imagination. Every action comes into our conscience and we use religion as the last excuse when no other answer makes sense. God is unexplainable, imperceivable, for only through true faith can you believe. Only through true faith can you ever hope to see the light. If we choose not to use religion as our excuse, to say, "I do what I do to be the best that I can be so that not only I, but you too, may be happy." I take responsibility for every last one of my actions.
For I am the accountable one.
My morals are based on how I want to be treated for I do unto others as I would have them do unto me. Not so that I can live free in heaven. Not so that this mythical being of light can smile, but so that we, all of us here together on this earth can survive together. With and for each other. In unison, in happiness. So that we can choose our own path no matter what that maybe. No matter where it may lead. For now is all we have and we can't hold back the nature of ourselves. *We* cannot hide from the world that which makes us human. Remove those last fig leaves and look not in shock (nor shame) but in wonderment and awe for we are all the same beautiful creatures regardless the nature of our shell be it black, white, green, disabled, crippled, deformed, or only half formed. We don't choose the nature of our shell so why should we be judged by it? What we do choose, is to live. To say I am alive and that is all. I eat because I am hungry and I like the sweet taste of tender meat's juices oozing between the dead muscles of a cow cooked medium rare as I gnaw it between my incisors. I breath because I am an organism like those green trees sharing with me their life. Life is about living so why stop at religion? Although we all know that

perishing will be our final debut in this play on life, we fear to know the exact time the crimson curtain shall fall and we become what our ancestors are now for we truly know not what that may be. Be it nothing, or that entity in our dreams that floats beyond the tear streaked clouds that our preachers and missionaries, priests and Rabbi, monks and medicine men, have proclaimed to house the strongest man who always was, is, and shall be. Regardless what you believe we are all here. Right now in this moment and this is all we really know. Don't leave your life up to chance. There is no need for excuses.

We are all the same and there is nothing wrong with that.

A new day is awakened to by an old mind. A mind hazed, a mind dazed. These are the days for the future. Every day is the next stage of constant evolution, constant revolution. The things we seek may or may not be found - these are the questions that all men have, and soon, will be answered. My hand writes not answers only prepares the mind for what could be if all goes well in the soul. We are not here to know. We are here to do, or do not. So many people assuming they have the answers only to prove that they don't even understand the questions. Why must we be as we are? Because that is how we are - there is no real reason to know - knowledge is but a mild sedation from reality where we can feel comfortable in being because for those moments in which we think we know we forget to question and that is when we become free. And why should we be free? For freedoms sake. For the simple purpose of being as we are for that is the definition of freedom. The only reason to be is to be. The only way to truly be is to live free. That is why I write, why I question, why I fight. So that I may be as I am and to see myself for what I truly am. I do what I can, I'm just a man. Do much do I? Nay – but at least I can say that is the path I am on. We all have our paths and far be it for me to judge. May your path lead you right, teach you right, hold you tight, and help you sleep at night. My path is my burden and I embrace it with open arms as it splits my back. Sympathy should you feel? No not at all. These are the decisions I make. After all this is my life that I'm living. I have chosen my burdens because they are who I am. Your burdens may trouble you, remember that the destination is waiting patiently for your arrival no matter how hard the path becomes remember that you are going where you want to go if you know it yet or not. Don't look at my life and say I have wronged for you have not seen me at my finish line yet. Do not look at my life and say that my path is your path for we all have our own unique destination. All you can really do is look at my life and see what might work for you or what helps you better understand your own path. Take from life anything you can to help you along your way. But, always remember to walk your own path with your head held high for that is how it is meant to be.

I'm not proud of what I've done.

If all the angels in heaven sing their praise to me for my deeds I'd not be proud of what I've done. I'm not proud of playing the creator. I'm not proud of pretending to be god. Making immoral decisions amidst moral convictions, I say, I'm not proud.

But I am proud of who I am.

Of where I stand today and I'm proud to say that I'm not proud of what I've done. I stand here as a poet proud. My voice and words coming out loud. I shout and I scream for with you I share my dreams. Greed knows no bounds in my heart. I will not hide from your eyes these things that I have seemed to see. For they are the embodiment of me.

Poetry sets me free.

I can say who I am and you may or may not understand. From you this I would never demand but listen, yes, I say there shall be no other way. I give to you of my life so that you may learn but you may say that you care not to hear, and I say, have you nothing left to learn? Can you learn nothing from me? That is yet to be seen, but you will never know 'til your ears become keen and the stories have left their mark. And if in that moment you learn nothing then I will bow and worship you for only a God knows all my tales and can learn nothing form my screaming crying wails.

No more of a man am I then you.

Your stories have the power to teach as well. And when you stand tall and tell all what you are hiding the most then I shall listen and take into my ghost the pieces of you you are willing to share. The pieces that you are willing to bare.

And so I dare you.

Tell me your stories, for I long to hear the beauty of words.

You may not have ever really read what I write because you may not like what you see. But on these pages is the true and pure me. This is my domicile in which I am free. No lies can I speak only truth be known in moving marks of language constantly changing and turning with the tides of the mind. How free without agreement does it really seem? Not free enough without a touch. With no ear to hear, to lips to laugh, no eyes to smile, no heart to beguile. But alone and free seemingly so it be for now, for me. Does it really matter if questions are answered or answers questioned.

I guess not because silence remains without refrain or re-framing. Like a picture put into words, the re-framed language of today becomes the truth in tomorrow's sorrow because one believed and agreed and said it is so.

Sow your own reaping that seeps from fresh grown souls but fear not the reaper who has grown old. He who falters, falters at will for all things of the will are willed by he who will. And if he won't then he will not and it his will that was lost. There is only a chance when you merely try and only success when you will success. And then you say with a question mark "but why do you tell these tales when all men know already?" Because all men are not listening. Their hearts, 'tis true, know as much but their minds askew think anew of times as if they had changed so much that truth could be forgotten as if it applied not to you, nor them or any friend in this day and age where memories are only lost within the pages.

Is your book complete when you close the cover or did you forget a chapter or two?

Complete your work and be satisfied.

And always be happy to say,

you have lived your life.

Thanx

If you've made it this far, then I probably owe you the greatest thanks. I didn't write the poetry and prose in this book for it to be read. However I'm glad that finally perhaps, people will read it. I hope you enjoy it as much as I do. I do want to offer thanx to a lot of people and more then I can name. I've had much help in my life including encouragement, support, or even just the borrowing of ears for a spell. Thanx to all those I cannot name for privacy or sheer forgetfulness, or for the sake of brevity.

For those I can name. I'd like to give special thanks to Nate M. at Cannon Coffee for providing an environment where poetry can be reborn and new artists can be discovered. I might not have been 'discovered' at your shop, but the fire was rekindled. Thanx to all the artists that attend the open mics for listening and encouraging me when I had given up hope on ever writing again. Thanx goes out to my 'pops' Jan, for being the father I always knew you were. Thanx to my 'ma' Brenda for never giving up on me, for loving me through thick and thin and for caring to talk more than I know how to do. Thanx to my sisters, Saskia and Asenath and my extended family for their love and support and for all that I learned from them. Special thanx to the Adams family for always treating me as one of their own.
Thanx Etta for your love, encouragement, all the good you bring to the world and for trusting a complete stranger when it seemed no one else would.
Thanx to so many more people that I wish I could name. You know who you are.

And a thank you and honorable mention to Nathan West for his incredible artwork, his complete willingness to fight an impossible deadline and put together this book cover as well as promotional fliers for this book's release. Many, many thanx.

To the readers of this work,
my humblest and most appreciated thanx.
Thanx again.

To all, Much love.